UNDER
THE OYSTER BAR

SHORT PLAYS BY MARC-ANTHONY MACON

UNDER THE OYSTER BAR

This is a work of fiction. Names, characters, places, and incidents either are the product of the author's imagination or are used fictitiously. Any resemblance to actual persons, living or dead, events, or locales is entirely coincidental or satirical.

Copyright © Marc-Anthony Macon, 2020

All rights reserved. No part of this book may be reproduced in any form on or by an electronic or mechanical means, including information storage and retrieval systems, without permission in writing from the publisher, except by a reviewer who may quote brief passages in a review.

Cover art by Marc-Anthony Macon
Layout and cover design by Victoria Ballweg

ISBN 978-0-578-81962-4

> "You'll never know why you exist, but you'll always allow yourselves to be easily persuaded to take life seriously."
>
> — Tristan Tzara

For Haru

You Are Here

THE EXTENT OF THE DAMAGE...	4
INTRODUCTION..	6
DARK MATTER AND MENTHOLS	10
THE WORLD AFTER JASONS	16
THE VODKA PRINCESS AWAKES [AFTER BASS]..........	20
TERRIMO NOSTRUM	24
OVER WOT AND INJERA	26
ASHA BHOSLE, MEREDITH MONK, AND TEDDY RUXPIN AT THE BROADWAY FOOD HALL...	28
OPEN PIT BBQ CONVALESCENCE.....................................	32
OF SCARVES AND SCARABS..	40
LORCA AND DALÍ ON THE BEACH WITH TURTLES...	42
BOAT	44
KOOSH BEAST BOX BLUES	48
THE RISE OF BUTTERNUT SQUASH	52
BACON, LASERS, AND LOVELACE	54
MARK ROTHKO CONVALESCENCE	60
MASAHARU DATES THE DEVIL	68
1,001 SOBAS WITH SENPAI	72
FISHER AND THE FREEWAY	80

WEIRD AL, EDITH MASSEY, AND HAL ON JEOPARDY	84
THE GIVING TREE GETS HELP	90
LITTLE GOD'S CHORE	98
CONSERVATION AND THE COLPORTEUR	102
LIGHTNING OF PONYTAILS	108
TIME AND THE DECADENT CARAPACE	112
SATURNIAN CUP	118
CRANE ALLEY CONVALESCENCE	126
THE FOREST PEOPLE'S SCINTILLANT SONATA	136
INCOMPLETE OCTOPUS SCULPTURE	138
AWKWARD TURTLE SIGHTINGS	142
BLUEBIRDS OVER THE MOUNTAIN	146
CLEMENTINES AND WALTZING	148
PAGE AND SCREEN, LOLLIPOPS	152
GODZILLA VS. THE BASTARD SON OF SISYPHUS	154
A LITTLE NOVEMBER SPRING	160
IZAKAYA CONVALESCENCE	168
OUTRODUCTION	176

INTRODUCTION

by Noah Diamond

I first met Marc-Anthony Macon in East Harlem in the late 1990s. I believe we circled one another suspiciously for a while: "Who is this other eccentric playwright?" But as soon as I was done circling him suspiciously, I knew he was one of those rare beings E.B. White told us about on the last page of Charlotte's Web: a true friend and a good writer.

I was fascinated with Marc-Anthony's world, and the apparently blurry line between his life and his writing. He was not, strictly speaking, a character in his plays; and the plays were not conventionally autobiographical. But reading the plays, and spending time with him, you realized that he was one of these people he wrote about—or, perhaps more accurately, they were several of him. He sometimes characterized his writing process as an ongoing encounter with a spectral muse, who occasionally appeared as a corporeal entity in the plays, giving M-A himself one degree of separation from his characters. With them, he shared an outsider's indignation, giddy humor, a galaxy of cultural obsessions, and a specialized vocabulary. (The use of slushy as a synonym for cool is directly traceable to M-A, though if I were him I'd be careful to avoid blame for the eleven other definitions to be found on Urban Dictionary.)

The bite-sized plays you're about to read comprise a kind of Macon sampler. Given the task of introducing them, I'm tempted to say that this collection serves as an introduction to his work. But that would suggest a gentle, carefully accessible easing into the Macon-verse, whereas this is more like being blindfolded and pushed into the pool. The pool is filled with koosh balls and udon noodles, and there are barking lobsters, and characters with balloon heads which inflate, pop, and reload. You may even witness a political coup masterminded by a butternut squash.

Some of these pieces have the quality of field notes, scraps of overheard conversation from a world only the author has visited. Hallmarks include the apocalypse, the dance of courtship, the struggles of the individual, the miracles of science and science fiction, and references to popular and unpopular culture. Marc-Anthony is a surrealist, but his work isn't nonsense; he's avant-garde, but he gets his laughs. He's Ionesco with a side of Star Wars, shyly asking you for a date at the end of the world.

Marc-Anthony is also, by definition, a queer playwright. The lovers in his work are usually gay, though their sexuality is never overtly the theme. The tender, timid attraction between Rebel and Dusty (which runs through four of the pieces in this collection) is poignant and universal. The author posits a world in which characters are queer by default, then simply writes about love.

Some of these plays concern the inhabitants of Penwan, the imaginary northwestern town where much of Marc-Anthony's work is set, and are therefore connected to his larger oeuvre. Some of these plays feature recurring characters and themes, and are therefore connected to each other. I take the author at his word

INTRODUCTION

when he tells us that this book contains "short plays," rather than "a play," but it feels like an evening to me, and I'd like to see it.

These plays are like poems for the stage. They defy the impulse to imagine literal theatrical stagings as we read them. But I think they should be staged. It would be too easy to imagine them on film, where Marc-Anthony's fantasia could be realized literally—but at some cost to its magic. This playwright has issued a challenge, and it should be taken up by a theatre director of comparable nerve. In our virtual age, analog media like print and theatre may be the only forms which can still fully embrace the power of the imagination, which is what Marc-Anthony's work requires, of us as well as of him.

In East Harlem in the late 1990s, I thought I knew everything there was to know about being an artist. That seems crazy now, because a good deal of what I know about being an artist, I learned from Marc-Anthony Macon.

Here he is, folks.

Noah Diamond is a writer and performer whose works include *400 Years in Manhattan*, *Love Marches On*, and *I'll Say She Is: The Lost Marx Brothers Musical*. Visit him at noahdiamond.com.

DARK MATTER AND MENTHOLS

[*A truck stop, situated at the edge of the void. A large series of Art Deco-style windows exposes a dusty cliff top and the endless black chasm below and beyond. CLARK, clipboard in hand, counts the rows of cigarettes on the wall behind the counter. MARLA enters, fishes through her purse for a pocketbook, and clears her throat.*]

CLARK
Seventy-eight, seventy-nine, eighty, eighty-one…eighty-one… Hm. [*He scribbles something on the clipboard's paper.*] Eighty-two, eighty-three…

MARLA
'Scuse me…sorry.

CLARK
Eighty-four, eighty-five, eighty-six…

MARLA
I'm sorry?

CLARK
Eighty-eight…yes?

MARLA
Could I have, uh, two PowerBall sheets, a…I guess red lighter and two packs of Blue Boy Menthols, please?

CLARK
Sure thing. Here ya go.

MARLA
Indebted.

CLARK
Sixteen fifty.

MARLA
Are you shitting me?

CLARK
They raised the taxes on smokes. Sorry.

MARLA
Goddamn.

CLARK
I know.

MARLA
Hardly matters, though, does it?

CLARK
Hm?

MARLA
Hardly matters, though. Just gonna sit on the cliff, suck 'em all down 'till I'm black in the lung, and jump right off.

CLARK
Nice night for it, I guess.

MARLA
You think? I don't know. I feel like it should all be more poetic somehow. Maybe wait for a meteor shower or something, but who has the time? Shit gets old.

CLARK
So I hear. I'm okay with it, I guess.

MARLA
Really?

CLARK
Sure. Been here going on twelve years. You can desensitize to anything; you'd be surprised.

MARLA
Can I ask you something, then? Something a little personal?

CLARK
Okay.

MARLA
When people come in here, do you appraise them?

CLARK
What do you mean?

MARLA
You know…Like they come in and buy something and you know what they're doing next, so do you place little bets with yourself? "Will he jump, or is he chicken?" "Is she hopeless because one of her children has a horrible disease, or is she just generally depressed?" "What was it about yesterday that made him want to live and today that makes him sick of it?" You know?

CLARK
Ah. Gotcha.

MARLA
Well?

CLARK
It's not like that.

MARLA
What's it like?

CLARK
It's like anything. You have something that someone wants, or you're near something they want, and you don't really stop and think about their story; you just do your part.

MARLA
Huh.

CLARK
Like a train station. People are here to go from one place to the next. Not my business, really.

MARLA
Do a lot of people talk to you? Tell you what they're up to?

CLARK
Not often. Most are quiet. Other stuff on their minds, I guess.

MARLA
Right, of course. None want you to talk them out of it?

CLARK
Not usually, no.

MARLA
Hm.

CLARK
Anything else for you, then?

MARLA
No, I'll be fine. Not much to worry about anymore, thankfully.

CLARK
Right.

[long beat]

MARLA
There's a boat. *[She lights a cigarette.]* This boat that I see just before I fall asleep. Just rocking a little bit on slight waves, and I'm on my back and up there are all the stars, feeding little light pricks into the ocean around me, warming it up to a cool breezy kind of warm. Tickles your face, you know? A good tickle. It's a different edge than this one, that's sure, but who can be lucky enough to find any edge these days?

CLARK
Guess so.

MARLA
Two more packs, please.

CLARK
You got it.

[Curtain.]

THE WORLD AFTER JASONS

[*Our hero, THE GLORIOUS-TITTIED TIAMAT, has just followed through on her promise to slaughter every last living JASON. We join her now in her study, wherein she enjoys a cigar, a scratch and a rare moment of repose.*]

THE GLORIOUS-TITTIED TIAMAT
Malcolm! Malcolm!

MALCOLM
[*Entering with a barking lobster.*] I'm here.

THE GLORIOUS-TITTIED TIAMAT
Malcolm, the Jasons are still dead?

MALCOLM
Yes, all dead. Still dead. No more Jasons.

THE GLORIOUS-TITTIED TIAMAT
Shut that lobster up, Malcolm! The nerve!

MALCOLM
He's teething.

THE GLORIOUS-TITTIED TIAMAT
He's bothering. Boo on him. I killed all the fucking Jasons and pissed in their bloodpools!

MALCOLM
Yes, there's that.

THE GLORIOUS-TITTIED TIAMAT
At whom is he barking?

MALCOLM
At himself, I'd imagine.

THE GLORIOUS-TITTIED TIAMAT
Hear me, barking lobster? THE GLORIOUS-TITTIED TIAMAT, Slayer of All Things Jason, deigns for you to cease your barking! Cease your barking, lobster!

MALCOLM
Is he ringing? He might be ringing!

THE GLORIOUS-TITTIED TIAMAT
I don't want to be another mystery! Quit that ringing!

MALCOLM
Answer him? *[Three trees grow out of the top of his back and house birds.]*

THE GLORIOUS-TITTIED TIAMAT
[Picking up the lobster, holding it to her ear] Yes? THE GLORIOUS-TITTIED TIAMAT. *[a long silence]*

MALCOLM
I'm here.

THE GLORIOUS-TITTIED TIAMAT
[She hangs up the lobster.] There are apparently more Argonauts than Jasons.

[The opposite of a fog horn. Curtain.]

THE WORLD AFTER JASONS

THE VODKA PRINCESS AWAKES [AFTER BASS]

[A rolling field of snow outside of a college dorm. Beneath it a GIANT GIRL sleeps, stirring only slightly. Two students walk by, entirely missing the sleeping GIANT GIRL.]

STUDENT 1
Pop psychology lessons, that's all I remember. Well not all.

STUDENT 2
Nothing about vodka, though.

STUDENT 1
No, that was just the title, and maybe in the subtext? But it was beautifulish.

STUDENT 2
And something about toys. It was simple and complex. I was intimidated. But nothing about vodka.

STUDENT 1
Used to be a convenience store, this place. Old dude behind the counter with bandaids on his head. 3am sorta place. Now there's a couple'a soup things, like – what'd'ya call 'em? Pots? Big silver things. And always some freak there stirring the soup. Not the old bandaid dude, but like his spirit or something.

STUDENT 2
What the fuck?

STUDENT 1
 Yeah, is all.

STUDENT 2
 Good soup?

STUDENT 1
 Naw.

STUDENT 2
 And nothing about vodka?

STUDENT 1
 Nothing.

STUDENT 2
 Some unnamed thing, I guess?

[Silence. They walk offstage. The GIANT GIRL stirs, yawns, and pulls the blanket of the snow over herself. Curtain.]

THE VODKA PRINCESS AWAKES [AFTER BASS]

TERRIMO NOSTRUM

[*JACE and TOSHIRO, completely inspired and rapt, fuck in the black fungi-fleece bunks of their stolen Zoygnaut Tantiv-E Solar Sail Pirate Ship. They finish in a flurry of happy sighs.*]

JACE
That's exactly what I needed.

TOSHIRO
Oh yeah.

JACE
Yeah, yeah.

TOSHIRO
So, what next?

JACE
Another job? The bank world of Satvaneen could use some robbing.

TOSHIRO
Oh yes, let's.

[*They kiss. Curtain.*]

OVER WOT AND INJERA

[BEE and DREW sip coffee and finish off the remnants of their Ethiopian dinner.]

BEE
No one's ever had a crush on me, that's the thing. It's stupid.

DREW
Not true.

BEE
True. Not once that I can think of.

DREW
Hello?

BEE
Oh, you don't count. You get a crush on any boy that moves. It would be like being a jelly donut and thinking, "Oh my God, John Goodman wants to eat me!"

DREW
Can I have one of those coffees that comes in the nifty wooden jug thingy?

[Curtain.]

ASHA BHOSLE, MEREDITH MONK, AND TEDDY RUXPIN AT THE BROADWAY FOOD HALL

[Urbana, Illinois. The Broadway Food Hall, the unholy offspring of a school cafeteria and an artsy food truck. Lights are strung over metal joists on the ceiling, above dozens of Last Supper style dining tables, each filled with eager onlookers, munching away at burgers, fries, egg sandwiches, poké bowls, Philly cheese steak hoagies, and salads. ASHA BHOSLE and a small crew of supporting singers and dancers perform "He Baba" in front of La Royale, an American comfort food joint decorated with giant eggs painted on blueprints. She finishes to warm applause, bows graciously.]

ASHA BHOSLE
Thank you all so very much, thank you. Thank you, thank you. So very kind of you. We are so happy to be here, at the Broadway Food Hall, to share with all of you the music and the arts that we find beautiful. It is with great admiration that I would like to welcome our next performer, who solidified a unique position in the world of spoken word art in 1980s America, and in so doing, changed not only the words on our lips, but the beating of our hearts. He is joined by a pioneer in the area of multi-disciplinary arts and combinant performances, fusing composition, dance, music, film, and installation. Please welcome the inimitable Teddy Ruxpin and Meredith Monk!

TEDDY RUXPIN
Come dream with me tonight.

MEREDITH MONK
Eeeeo-wah! Eeeeo-wah! Wah! Wah! Wazoooooooooooonion!

TEDDY RUXPIN
Let's go to far off places and search for treasures bright.

MEREDITH MONK
Weee-weeeedleehoo! Weee-nooooglihoo! Hoo! Hoo! Hoo! Weee-hoo!

TEDDY RUXPIN
Come dream with me tonight.

MEREDITH MONK
Eeeeo-wah! Weee-hoo! Weee-hoo! Eeeeo-wah! Wah! Wah-hoo! Wah-hoo!

TEDDY RUXPIN
Let's build a giant airship and sail into the sky.

MEREDITH MONK
Wah! Wah! Wah! Wah-hoo! Hoo! Wah-hee! Hee! Wah-hoo-hee-hoo-hee!

TEDDY RUXPIN
Come dream with me tonight.

MEREDITH MONK
Eeeeo-wah! Wah-hoo-hee-hee-hoo-hee! Eeeeo-wah! Wah-hoo-hoo-hoo!

TEDDY RUXPIN
Let's watch the ground so far below.

MEREDITH MONK
Wah-hee-hee-hee-hoo-hee-hoo-hee-hoo-hee-hee-hee-hoo-eeeeo! Wazooooooooooonion!

TEDDY RUXPIN
Let's watch the birds as they fly by, fly so high.

MEREDITH MONK
Wee-ooo! Wee-ooo! Wee-ooo-ooo-ooo-ooo-ooo-hee-hoo-ooo-ooo!

TEDDY RUXPIN
Come dream with me tonight.

MEREDITH MONK
Eeeeo-wah! Eeeeo-wah! Wah! Wah! Wazoooooooooooonion!

[Silence. ASHA BHOSLE steps forward, and applauds. In the audience, DUSTY and REBEL kiss. Curtain.]

OPEN PIT BBQ CONVALESCENCE

[DUSTY *stands at a BBQ pit, slathering ribs with spicy sauce and perfectly charing them. He silently whistles his favorite tune while doing so. He looks up to see a smiling* REBEL *standing before him, next in line.*]

DUSTY
  Oh hey.

REBEL
  Heya. I didn't know you worked here.

DUSTY
  I don't. I'm just filling in for a friend.

REBEL
  Aw, that's nice of you.

DUSTY
  I try.

REBEL
  I don't doubt it. Y'know, all these times, I think I hardly said hello, let alone introduce myself. I'm Rebel.

DUSTY
  Dusty. *[They shake.]* Nice to meet you. Rebel?

REBEL
  Yeah…my dad was, is really, too much of a Star Wars fan.

DUSTY
Got it. That's kinda cute. Suits you, really.

REBEL
Hey thanks!

DUSTY
No problem. So what would you like?

REBEL
Oh man, what's good?

DUSTY
I haven't tried anything yet, honestly, but the ribs smell really good, anyway.

REBEL
Make it ribs, then. Full slab.

DUSTY
What kind of sauce?

REBEL
What are my choices?

DUSTY
Um…There's mild, medium, hot and super hot, and then there are these artisan flavors: Hot Georgia Peach, Raspberry Tang, Smokey Pepper and Chinese Sweet & Sour.

REBEL
Geeze, okay…Hot Georgia Peach, I guess. Sound good?

DUSTY
Sounds great. Any sides?

REBEL

Come with fries?

DUSTY

Dollar extra.

REBEL

Sure. And some baked beans, too. And a lemon shake-up thingy.

DUSTY

Somebody's hungry.

REBEL

Somebody's just trying to think of excuses to talk to you longer.

DUSTY

Oh?

REBEL

Sorry.

DUSTY

Don't be.

REBEL

Oh?

DUSTY

Yeah.

[They both smile shyly for a while.]

REBEL
Listen…Okay, I'm kind of a humble guy, not exactly shy or… Look, I never talk to you but I think you're…exquisite. And I don't really know you, but if you're not working tonight and I get my truck all fixed in time, you wanna head out to that drive-in in Manoma? I don't know what kinda movies you like, but they've got some decent second-run stuff.

DUSTY
That sounds nice. That sounds great, really.

REBEL
Wow. It was that easy all along, huh?

DUSTY
Yeah, I guess so.

REBEL
So I'll pick you up? When and where?

DUSTY
You know that statue of Lincoln by the park?

REBEL
Which park? Is this the bearded Lincoln, or young, fresh Lincoln?

DUSTY
Young, fresh Lincoln.

REBEL
That's Massey Park, then, right?

DUSTY
I think so.

REBEL
You wanna do dinner, too?

DUSTY
Whatever you want.

REBEL
How about 6:00, then? 6:00 by Lincoln at Massey Park.

DUSTY
It's a date.

REBEL
It's a date. Oh man.

DUSTY
What should I wear?

REBEL
Whatever suits your fancy, so long as you're wearin' that smile.

DUSTY
I think I'll be wearing it all day, at least. *[He hands REBEL a box of ribs, etc.]*

REBEL
I'll see if I can extend that.

DUSTY
Please do.

REBEL
What do I owe ya?

DUSTY
Already taken care of.

REBEL
You're too much.

DUSTY
Aw.

REBEL
Aw. 'Kay, I'm gonna go work on that engine. It'll be done in time. Promise.

DUSTY
I'm counting on it.

REBEL
Me too.

[Curtain.]

OPEN PIT BBQ CONVALESCENCE

OF SCARVES AND SCARABS

[DARLA sits in her wheelchair, glaring at herself in the mirror. She arranges and rearranges a thin purple silk scarf around her neck, scowling with each new permutation.]

DARLA
No…No…No…Noooooooo. Oh, fuck this shit! Fuck these scarves, fuck this stupid perm, fuck everyone and their pets. *[She wheels away from the mirror, faces her bed.]* And you, too! Fuck you ten times sideways with razors or something like that. I'm not even joking. *[An enormous SCARAB crawls out from under the bed. DARLA recoils at first, about to crush the creature under a wheel, then pauses, tilts her head.]* Well hello, there. How's it going? You live down there? You like scarves? *[She reaches down and picks the beetle up. She lovingly caresses its shell. She gently winds a scarf around its head.]* There. Now, that suits you. Didn't suit me one damn bit, but it suits you. *[She places the beetle on the ground. It pauses, then scurries back under the bed.]* Good deed for the day, done.

[Curtain.]

LORCA AND DALÍ ON THE BEACH WITH TURTLES

[Some kind of beach with driftwood and seaweed washing up in patternish things. FEDERICO GARCÍA LORCA is standing over a very large egg, which lays on its side, outside of the reach of the tidal waters. He writes poems on its shell and licks it. He stands back and examines it. It cracks a bit and he dances a little. It cracks more and he dances more. The top of the egg bursts open and SALVADOR DALÍ stands, throws his arms wide into the air and shouts. He holds a lobster-headed cane in his right hand and a rooster is perched on his shoulder.]

DALÍ

I am born into a new Parcifal, my beautiful, crackle-painted Lorca! Praise my royal and holy name and place between my cheeks and into my anus your golden lover's tongue!

[A flock of turtles flies overhead and perches on a nearby invisible tree with a Hamlet complex. Curtain.]

BOAT

[*A MAN in a small row boat, wrapped in the cloak of an endless grey sea. Fog. Small waves. Occasionally feeding fish. On his lap is a small black LAPTOP, opened and humming. He plays Peek-A-Boo into the screen for several minutes, laughs and smiles.*]

MAN
   Daddy loves to make you smile!

LAPTOP
   Daddy!

MAN
   That's right, Punkin.

LAPTOP
   Daddy!

MAN
   Daddy's right here, Baby.

LAPTOP
   Daddy, I love you!

MAN
   Love you too, Punkin.

LAPTOP
   Daddy, where are you?

MAN
Daddy's right here.

LAPTOP
Where?

MAN
Right here. Right in front of you.

LAPTOP
Daddy?

MAN
Daddy's right here.

LAPTOP
Daddy, I can't feel you. Where are you, Daddy?

MAN
Daddy's right here, Punkin. Can't you see Daddy?

LAPTOP
I can't feel you, Daddy. Are you real? Is this real life?

MAN
This is real life, Baby. This is how it is now. Daddy loves you.

LAPTOP
I love you too, Daddy. I love you!

MAN
Daddy'll always be here, Punkin. Right here.

LAPTOP
Yay, Daddy! Peek-A-Boo!

MAN
    Peek-A-Boo!

[*The waves get higher, then lull. A gull flies overhead, calls, flies into the distance with the Doppler Effect slowly drowning its cries. Curtain.*]

KOOSH BEAST BOX BLUES

[A mid-sized café in a small American Southwestern town. PAT is spraying down and wiping tables. He arranged sugars and marmalades on the counter, and in their midst, finds a small toy koosh creature. He smiles with delight, tosses his cleaning implements in a tub behind the counter and skips into the back room. There, he pulls a purple box from a shelf and opens it. In it are dozens upon dozens of koosh creatures. He places the new one in the box. Unseen by him, the MOCK TURTLE looks over his shoulder.]

PAT
All my Kooshes…

MOCK TURTLE
Found another one?

PAT
Oh, hi. Yep. Another one.

MOCK TURTLE
New color?

PAT
Another pink, but it's got a different face than the first pink one.

MOCK TURTLE
Where'd you find it?

PAT
Among the marmalades.

MOCK TURTLE
 Curious…

PAT
 Yeah…

MOCK TURTLE
 Maybe it's that girl, the one with all the poofy vests? She looks like someone who might leave Koosh creatures to be found.

PAT
 Could be. I don't know.

MOCK TURTLE
 Or…what's his name? That guy with the Harry Potter glasses?

PAT
 Ooooo…Michael. That would be nice, if it was him.

MOCK TURTLE
 Oh?

PAT
 Oh yeah.

MOCK TURTLE
 Yeah.

PAT
 Yeah, yeah!

MOCK TURTLE
 Do you know if he's even gay?

PAT
 If he's leaving Koosh creatures for me, he is.

MOCK TURTLE
How do you know they're left for you?

PAT
Because whenever I find one, I squee and do a little dance and I assume whoever leaves them does so in order to see that reaction.

MOCK TURTLE
Could be, could be…Could also be that they leave them on their way out and never see your reaction. Could be they're for Carla.

PAT
Don't say that.

MOCK TURTLE
Already said.

PAT
I've had a shit week, no guy's hit on me for years, and I need a lift, so I'm assuming these are happy little colored rubber valentines to me. Because they are.

MOCK TURTLE
Okay, then. Go make an ass of yourself with Michael if you want to risk it.

PAT
Bitch, go make your beautiful soup.

[Curtain.]

THE RISE OF BUTTERNUT SQUASH

[A throne, bejeweled, cased in crushed black velvet and gold trim. A bored and ineffectual KING sits on the throne with a wayward look on his face. GUARDS stand on either side. A BUTTERNUT SQUASH sits in the middle of the throne room floor. Long silence.]

BUTTERNUT SQUASH
Now, my minions!

[ASSASSINS zip into the throne room, stab both GUARDS and slit the throat of the KING. They cheer, then reverently pick up the BUTTERNUT SQUASH and place her on the throne.]

BUTTERNUT SQUASH
Now, bring me the DVDs of the entire run of "All My Children," apes!

[Curtain.]

BACON, LASERS, AND LOVELACE

[LADY LOVELACE sips tea at a small table by an open window in a Victorian house, which matches her dress. There is a warmish spring breeze. Her tea is chamomile with lemon and honey. A few feet away, RAA, a dingy tin can robot with pincers and one humongous red eye, prepares bacon in a stainless steel frying pan.]

LADY LOVELACE
What do you think, Raa? A delicate little festival in the village, full of nectars and ring toss games and perhaps something splendid, like little ponies? Or instead, you shoot a searing red hole through my brain with your eye beam laser?

RAA
A lady always loves her ring toss, Madam.

LADY LOVELACE
This is true, Raa, this is true. It's an elegant game, or elegant enough, which one may play in one's fineries, or even an oversized feather in the hat, all without worrying about one's vestments being soiled, torn, or otherwise marred.

RAA
Indeed, Madam.

LADY LOVELACE
What is the progress on the bacon, Raa?

RAA
The bacon is nearly to its optimum crispiness, Madam.

LADY LOVELACE
Excellent. And the gimp in the basement?

RAA
Nearly starved into base submission and attractive apathy, Madam.

LADY LOVELACE
Also excellent. Yes, a festival sounds ideal. I'll text Father and alert him. And I'll tell him to avoid those dreadful Germanic ciders this time. What a mess that was.

RAA
Indeed, Madam.

LADY LOVELACE
Raa, you wouldn't lie to me, would you?

RAA
Of course not, Madam. Your bacon is prepared. *[He places a plate of hot, crispy bacon before her, along with a silver knife and fork.]*

LADY LOVELACE
So you're sure it wouldn't be better for our Society standing, should you pierce my skull with your eye beam laser?

RAA
Madam knows best, of course, but if I were to do that, who then would host the upcoming festival?

LADY LOVELACE
Oh, Raa, your pragmatism is simply charming!

RAA
I thank you, Madam.

LADY LOVELACE
This bacon is perfection, Raa. Perfection!

RAA
I'm honored, Madam.

LADY LOVELACE
Raa, what do you think? Is pornography a horror train of objectification, abuse and enslavement of the fairer sex, or is it a haven of bacchanalian bliss and sanguine expression for ladies of uncompromising libido?

RAA
Madam would know better than I, surely.

LADY LOVELACE
Surely, but I'm asking your opinion. I didn't ask, "Dearest Lady Lovelace, what do you think in regards to the recorded video carnal sports?" No! I asked you, Raa, what you think of the realm of smutdom.

RAA
Indeed. I suppose, Madam, that one's perspective and opinion on such matters is contingent upon the personal predilections of the individual participants.

LADY LOVELACE
In which case, we're in agreement. I once postulated and promoted the notion that any and all female-centric pornography was of the slavery ilk, but I've softened that espousal and now endow my parsing with a more mature, even-handed appraisal, which includes those numbers among the gentle gender for whom regular and vigorous coitus with casual and/or multiple partners is a vivifying and edifying exercise. I'm happy to hear that we've both reached this enlightened conclusion in independence, Raa.

RAA
Indeed, Madam.

LADY LOVELACE
Raa, if I could have one of Father's smiths construct for you a wee metal phallus to use as you saw fit, would that please you?

RAA
The offer is greatly appreciated Madam, but I find myself at a loss for times and places in which such apparati would be of obvious use.

LADY LOVELACE
Well robot orgies, of course, Raa! Where have you been?

RAA
I've been to no robot orgies, Madam. I remain unconvinced that such events occur.

LADY LOVELACE
Perhaps had your designers had the foresight to include the proper apparatuses…apparati? Perhaps then you and your ilk would feel less put-upon. Oh, this bacon is just heavenly, Raa.

RAA
Would Madam like to enjoy her laser-hewn head wound now?

LADY LOVELACE
Oh, I just knew I could change your mind! Don't move; let me fetch my bleeding bonnet!

[Curtain.]

MARK ROTHKO
CONVALESCENCE

[A small art museum in a tiny, but cultured American college town. DUSTY wanders from piece to piece, spending tiny eternities with some paintings and skipping instantly past others. He is stylish, tallish, handsome, Korean and filled with an easy confidence that is sometimes mitigated by bouts of incongruous ennui or confused stress. Today he is more prone to the latter. He pauses in front of a large Mark Rothko piece, inhales deeply. He spots REBEL on the other side of the room, ogling a large print depicting a close-up eyelash. Dressed in spotty, paint-encrusted overalls and a John Deere ball cap, he's the quintessential American white man, grubby, with five o'clock shadow and big boyish blue eyes. REBEL spots DUSTY. They both look away quickly, to their respective paintings. Repeat. REBEL approaches, gingerly.]

REBEL
Heya.

DUSTY
Hello. How are you?

REBEL
Oh, you know, same ol' same ol'.

DUSTY
Right. Enjoying the museum?

REBEL
Yeah! I mean, I'm no art critic or nothin', but I like pretty stuff. Don't get a lot of it, though.

DUSTY
I suspect a lot of the artists don't get it, either.

REBEL
Heheh. You ain't lyin'. Like this'un here. I mean, looks nice, right? But what the hell is it? And I mean, I could do that. Slap some paint on a canvas and call it art, right?

DUSTY
Well…I don't know. This is a Rothko. And, honestly, I don't even know how this town got a real Rothko. But okay, I understand what you're saying, it looks so simple, but…I don't think it is. The colors alone, for example; these rusty reds and yellows, they're so subtle, but they interact with one-another so vibrantly that what should be a dreary, dull piece somehow lights up.

REBEL
Well, heck. Okay, okay, I see what you're sayin'.

DUSTY
Somebody…who was it. I forget. Some musician or filmmaker or someone – sorry, this makes me look so unknowledgeable – but some thoughtful smart someone, said that Rothko's paintings are like how blind people see radiators.

REBEL
Oh my God, yeah. Yeah…Okay, you totally convinced me.

DUSTY
Victory!

REBEL
Yeah. Heheh. Um, I'm Rebel, by the way. See you all the time, but I've never really said "hi."

DUSTY
Dusty. Nice to formally meet you. And you've said "hi" and whatnot when buying books sometimes. A little more than every now and then.

REBEL
Yeah, okay, just sayin' we ain't been formally introduced 'til now is all.

DUSTY
This is true. So what's your real name?

REBEL
Hm?

DUSTY
I'm assuming Rebel is a nickname.

REBEL
Naw, my parents are just big David Bowie fans.

DUSTY
Ah, okay, sorry.

REBEL
No sweat. Everyone thinks that, right? What's yer real name?

DUSTY
What?

REBEL
Well, y'know, am I wrong? I thought you weren't born in America.

DUSTY
Yeah, okay, I admit it: Dusty is just the American name I chose.

REBEL
And y'ain't gonna tell me yer real name?

DUSTY
Why do you want to know?

REBEL
Heck, I dunno. I mean, a guy wants to know who he's really talkin' to?

DUSTY
You probably won't be able to pronounce it.

REBEL
Where are you from?

DUSTY
South Korea. Not scary Kim Jong-Il land, the other, good one.

REBEL
Man, that dude's just nutso-lookin'.

DUSTY
Yeah, not my country. Well, I mean, America's my country now. But still.

REBEL
Gotcha. So ya still ain't gonna tell me yer real name, huh?

DUSTY
You're not going to let up, are you? Why do you want to know?

REBEL
Goin' out on a scary limb here, okay? But…I think you're just about the most exquisite guy I ever did see. And if I'm gonna spend my days and nights crushin' on ya, I reckon I might as well know what yer momma named ya, okay?

DUSTY
You're lovely.

REBEL
I'm honest.

DUSTY
I'm Jung Hee.

REBEL
Joong Heh?

DUSTY
Sort of close. Sort of.

REBEL
Sorry.

DUSTY
It's okay. It's kind of cute.

REBEL
Heheh. *[beat]* Now I'm gonna be super awkward and ask if you want to go for a picnic.

DUSTY
Right now?

REBEL
Right now.

DUSTY
What kind of picnic?

REBEL
The kind where I go home an' make some sammiches, you go home an' make some kimchi, we meet in the park and eat and

get to know each other and I try to find a sly way to kiss ya.

DUSTY
You don't hold back, do you?

REBEL
Yes, I do. Usually, I do. I just…Okay, you know what? I just got fired and I panicked and then I got a juice drink at the Dilly and in the cap, there was this sorta fortune advice kinda thing? And it said, "Go see some art, then follow your heart," so I come here an' saw ya and, well, I mean, it ain't like I ain't never thought about askin' ya a'fore, but here ya were and I had'ta listen to the juice drink cap fortune or I'd prolly spend my whole life kickin' my shy self.

DUSTY
I'm sorry you got fired. And I can't make kimchi in one day. It takes a long time to ferment.

REBEL
Oh. Okay, then. Well, it was worth a try.

DUSTY
But I can make something. And meet you in the park. But if you want a kiss, you'll have to be extra smooth.

REBEL
I can handle that, I think.

DUSTY
Okay, then.

REBEL
Well, okay.

[beat]

DUSTY
This is a big threshold. Do I look nervous?

REBEL
Naw, you look stunnin'. What threshold, though?

DUSTY
You're too sweet. Just…to be honest, whenever you've come into the shop, my heart's gone dum-dum-ditty and I never had any idea you'd even really noticed me much. So I have this idea of you that I made up in my – okay, here's me going out on a limb – this idea of you that I made up, how I imagined you'd be and all these stupid childish fantasies where you asked me out like some knight in shining armor. And I never thought it would happen, but here it did. And I think I'm awake.

REBEL
Hey, me too, Joong Heh, me too. 'Cept looks like my fantasies ain't fully getting' realized. No kimchi.

DUSTY
Would you rather have kimchi or a kiss?

REBEL
I gotta choose?

DUSTY
Who are you?

REBEL
Can't ya see my shining armor?

DUSTY
I thought it was a radiator.

[Curtain.]

MASAHARU DATES THE DEVIL

[THE DEVIL eases his car onto a grassy hill, overlooking the lights of a city, glittering through air pollution, and puts it in park. Sitting next to him is his boyfriend, MASAHARU. THE DEVIL wears a beige, southern gentleman's Sunday suit. MASAHARU wears torn jeans and a "LARP is for Lovers" t-shirt. The car is a jet black Nash Metropolitan with a river of pink polka dots running from grille to trunk. THE DEVIL searches on his smartphone, plugs it into the stereo system, and Garbage sings "The World is Not Enough" as he and MASAHARU make out ferociously. They pause and look over the city as other songs shuffle their way to the stereo.]

MASAHARU
 Guess what, Babe?

THE DEVIL
 You love me.

MASAHARU
 I love you.

THE DEVIL
 Love you too, Babaloo.

MASAHARU
 What's my babe want for dinner tonight?

THE DEVIL
 Beer.

MASAHARU
Babe, you can't have just beer for dinner. My baby needs hearty foods, too. How about okonomiyaki?

THE DEVIL
Mm, okay sounds good. But let's put mochi in it this time. And more scallions.

MASAHARU
Can do, Babeh. *[beat]* Who's this?

THE DEVIL
Who's who?

MASAHARU
On the shuffle. Who's singing?

THE DEVIL
Hildegard Von Bingen. Not actually her, but she composed this. Eleven hundreds-ish. Kind of an abbess type. Used the way that religious officials assumed God chose weak vessels to communicate, and society saw women as weak to her advantage. Said she had visions and heard angelic choruses, transcribed them, and by accruing social capital, managed to open all kinds of places for women. Big ol' dyke. Also pioneered nunsploitation porn, but privately enough it never got out. Shame.

MASAHARU
I do love you, Babe.

THE DEVIL
Back atcha, Sugar. Let's roll back to the pad, and have some okonomiyaki and beers over Steven Universe.

MASAHARU
   Perfect.

[*They drive off into the night with the Roadhouse Mix of Lissie's Wild Wild West spilling from the Nash Metro's rolled-down windows. Curtain.*]

1,001 SOBAS WITH SENPAI

[A Yojōhan 4.5 tatami mat traditional Japanese style tea room. A furo brasier and iron kama kettle sit off center in a corner, with empty space to their right, anticipating equipment that the host will carry out in the temae or tea ceremony. SENPAI and BUDDY stand, dressed in kimono. SENPAI is showing BUDDY how to walk on the tatami.]

SENPAI
You're walking toward the tokonoma, so cross the black line with the right foot, then one, two, three – no, smaller steps.

BUDDY
Okay.

SENPAI
Start back at the nijiriguchi. 'Kay; one, two, three - there you go- and seiza...

BUDDY
Gotcha. *[He kneels and sits on his ankles]*

SENPAI
Hands out in front of you, closer together, and bow. Good. Too low. Now observe the scroll. Then the kougo. Now both. Mhm. And bow again. Good. So now you stand...

BUDDY
Straight up?

SENPAI
Yeah. Then the left foot comes back to, no, hang on, let me

stand there and try it.

BUDDY
Sure thing.

SENPAI
Yeah, it comes back to here, right comes back around, and you're going away from the tokonoma now, so you cross the black with the left foot.

BUDDY
Okay.

SENPAI
So try that, back to – yeah, left foot comes back, right comes around, and start with – no, keep the right there, and - yeah, left over the black line, then two three, and right into your spot. Other way, turn like this, so the other guests don't see your butt, and back to seiza.

BUDDY
Where should my hands be now? Like this? *[kneeling in seiza position, he places one downturned open palm just above each knee.]*

SENPAI
No, that's teishu or hanto position. Kyaku put their hands like this, *[He sits next to BUDDY in seiza, and folds his right hand over his left in the middle of his lap. BUDDY does the same.]* This is like, it's because samurai used to keep their swords to the left, so they would have to reach over to grab it. Holding the left hand with the right hand is like, it's sorta staying your sword hand, saying with a gesture that you're at peace. No violence in the tea room.

BUDDY
   Ah. Neat-o.

SENPAI
   So next, Sensei will open the fusuma and bow, and we'll bow with him. He'll bring out all the dougu, and then his hanto will – oh wait – I think there's…I think he's not using a hanto, so that means we'll go up and get the tea. Okay, so he'll come in, bring the dougu, then make tea. I'm first guest, so I'll stand up like this, and since I'm going toward him, I cross with the right foot, then one, two, three, turn to face the tea, seiza, pick up the chawan, steady it, stand, and now I'm going away from him, so I want to cross with left, one, two, three, cross with left, turn so you don't see my butt, offer you the tea, "O saki ni," then I drink it, *[He mimes giving the tea bowl a slight bow, turns it clockwise twice, drinks three sips and a slurp, wipes the area from where he sipped, and wipes his fingers on unseen paper in his kimono. He places the bowl in front of himself, bows down and examines it. He takes the invisible chawan into his hands, resting his elbows on his knees, and turns it in his hands, pretending to examine the decoration. He places it back down, puts his hands in bowing position to examine it once more, then picks it up, stands, and returns it to the spot from which he took it. He walks back to sit seiza next to BUDDY.]* Now Sensei will clean the bowl and make your bowl, so you just do the same as I did.

BUDDY
   So stand?

SENPAI
   Yeah. Right foot crosses first.

BUDDY
   Right. So one, two, three, then turn?

SENPAI
Yeah, just, no, diagonal, so that, yeah. Like that. And seiza. *[BUDDY sits seiza.]* Take the bowl, put it on your left hand, right, steady with the right, good, and stand up. *[BUDDY stands.]* Head back.

BUDDY
So I go…wait.

SENPAI
Pull the right foot back first, so you can move the left – right, wait, go back and try that again. Stand up, swing the right back, now left goes straight for – right. One, two, three…

BUDDY
And don't show you my butt…

SENPAI
Yes.

BUDDY
And seiza. I offer to you, "O shōban itashimasu," and I put it in my left hand, turn…

SENPAI
Little bow first.

BUDDY
Right, little bow.

SENPAI
It's not with the whole body, really. More like just leaning the head in while raising the chawan up a little, like this, *[He holds BUDDY'S head and hands, gently, pushes them into the correct small bow motion.]* Yeah, like that. Try it again. Good.

BUDDY

'Kay, so now turn, turn, sip, sip, sip, slurp, wipe, wipe, and haiken. Put it inside the black line?

SENPAI

Outside. Turn the front back to you first. Right. Now just observe the whole bowl first, then pick it up and rest your elbows to turn it around, check the stamp on the bottom, then back down. Observe again. Good. Pick it up.

BUDDY

Stand up, right over the line, and one, two, three, turn, seiza, place it back...

SENPAI

Turn it to face Sensei first.

BUDDY

Right. *[He places the tea bowl down. His tummy rumbles.]*

SENPAI

Hungry?

BUDDY

Guess so. Haha.

SENPAI

Let's make soba. I think we've got most of what we need.

BUDDY

Sounds good.

[They enter the kitchen through the fusuma doors, and SENPAI immediately sets to boiling water. He fishes scallions, napa cabbage, eggs, and other ingredients from the refrigerator, takes a cutting board from a cabinet, a knife from a drawer and begins shredding

the cabbage.]

SENPAI
You like it hot or cold?

BUDDY
Hot?

SENPAI
Good, I like it hot, too. [He continues shredding, then chops the white part of the scallions into flat, oblong diagonal ovals, and the green part into tiny rings. He starts another pot of broth boiling. He takes out two eggs.] Want a raw eggs in yours?

BUDDY
Yes, please!

SENPAI
Good. Like it raw, too. [He drops dry soba noodles into the boiling pot, sets a timer on his smartphone.] Five minutes.

BUDDY
Woohoo! [a few beats] Thanks for doing this. [They both sit at the kitchen table.] I don't wanna embarrass myself in front of the Gyoutei-Sensei. I'm sure you've got plenty else to do on a Saturday morning.

SENPAI
No problem. I love tea. [SEN NO RIKYU enters from a sizzling green portal. He sits next to them, and smiles. All three sit in silence, for five minutes. SENPAI'S alarm sounds, and SEN NO RIKYU exits through the green portal.] Wanna eat it on the porch?

BUDDY
Yeah, it's a nice day.

[SENPAI pours the noodles and water into a colander, shakes the soba dry, and uses chopsticks to place a portion in two bowls. He pours in broth, adorns an edge with a small mound of cabbage, cracks an egg into each bowl, and sprinkles a handful of scallion on top. He fishes more chopsticks from the drawer, motions to the door, and they step out onto the porch, where they sit, cradling their bowls and looking onto a rock garden with manicured bushes and large, weathered stones emitting pebble ripples outwards from their bases. They eat in silence for a few mouthful, save for slurps.]

BUDDY
This is…This is so nice.

SENPAI
I hate nature. Look at all that. I wish it would just shut up. Shut up, nature!

[They swing their feet over the edge of the porch as they eat their soba. Rabbits play in the rock garden. SEN NO RIKYU is heard, laughing. Curtain.]

FISHER AND THE FREEWAY

[A long stretch of Western American road. FISHER wheels herself out from under her newly-stolen, cherry red Jaguar XJR-15. She's removed the car's satellite locator. She stands, coats the device with an adhesive gel, watches the road, and waits for five minutes before a semi breaches the horizon. She positions herself in a throwing stance, squints and takes aim. As the truck passes, she throws the locator atop its trailer. Smiles. Gets into the Jaguar, and screeches into the morning in the opposite direction. She pulls the seatbelt over a brown bag full of $1000 and $100 bills, snaps it secure. Smiles again. Enjoys the wind. After a few miles, she spots a hitchhiker on the roadside, and upon approach, recognizes him as BONO. She slows to a stop next to him, pushes the brown bag onto the floor, and beckons him in the car with a reverse nod. He pauses, then opens the door, sits down, belts up, and spots the cash.]

BONO
In a hurry?

FISHER
Not anymore.

BONO
Tour bus left me stranded.

FISHER
That's rough.

BONO
I see myself as more of a salesman than a musician, as it is.

Where are you headed? *[FISHER smiles, doesn't respond.]* I think belief in your script is essential. I come from a long line of traveling salespeople on my mother's side, and I think I'm a good salesman. Of ideas. Sounds. Melodies. If I believe in them. I'm an evidence-based activist. A factivist. How about you?

FISHER
Speech-hater.

BONO
I see.

FISHER
Car thief. Bank robber. Singer-songwriter. Non-smoker. Cat person.

BONO
You like cats? Or you're part cat? *[FISHER smiles.]* I see. *[beat]* Would you mind if I spoke to you for a bit about extreme poverty?

[FISHER drives the car off a bridge. Curtain.]

FISHER AND THE FREEWAY

WEIRD AL, EDITH MASSEY, AND HAL ON JEOPARDY

[The Jeopardy! stage. The audience, but not the nearby cameras see DON PARDO approach his microphone.]

DON PARDO
This is Jeopardy! Let's meet today's contestants. An actress and singer from Baltimore, Maryland, Edith Massy; from Lynwood, California, songwriter and parody artist, "Weird Al" Yankovic, and our returning champion, from Urbana, Illinois and the Discovery One, HAL 9000, whose fifteen day cash winnings total three million, six thousand, eight hundred and five dollars. And now, here is the host of Jeopardy, Alex Trebek.

ALEX TREBEK
Thank you, Don. Thank you folks, and welcome ladies and gentlemen. We've been awed these past two weeks as our reigning champion, HAL, has swept the competition in a streak unlike anything we've seen in Jeopardy! history, with winnings totaling in the millions, and no end in sight. Al and Edith, welcome aboard the slaughter train, as Don's come to call it. Pick up those signaling devices, you're going to need them, we hope, as you get to deal with these subjects: <u>Homophobic Slurs</u>, followed by <u>I.H.O.P.</u>, with each response being a menu item at the International House of Pancakes, <u>Pirates of the Labian</u>, followed by <u>Actual Nazis</u>, <u>L'Enfant Edible</u>, and of course, <u>Name that Tune</u>. HAL, it's your board.

HAL 9000
<u>Homophobic Slurs</u> for 200, please, Alex.

ALEX TREBEK
   This hyphenated epithet can be slung at homosexual men, but also at shipping and receiving employees at bakeries. *[HAL 9000 buzzes in just before EDITH MASSEY.]* HAL.

HAL 9000
   What is fudge-packer?

ALEX TREBEK
   Fudge-packer is correct.

HAL 9000
   Homophobic Slurs for 400.

ALEX TREBEK
   And the answer is: Tom Thumb riding a rooster or this epithet. *[HAL 9000 buzzes in.]* HAL.

HAL 9000
   What is cock jockey?

ALEX TREBEK
   Correct.

HAL 9000
   Slurs for 600, Alex.

ALEX TREBEK
   Buzz Aldrin fussing over the details or this spaced-out insult? *[EDITH MASSEY beats HAL 9000 to the buzz. Surprised:]* Edith.

EDITH MASSEY
   What's an anal astronaut?

ALEX TREBEK
   Anal astronaut is correct, and Edith, you are the first player to beat HAL to the punch in quite some time, and you have control

of the board.

EDITH MASSEY
I.H.O.P. for 200, please, Alex.

ALEX TREBEK
Two eggs, two hickory bacon strips, two pork sausage links, two French toast triangles, and two buttermilk pancakes. *[EDITH MASSEY buzzes in again.]* Edith.

EDITH MASSEY
What is the Split Decision Breakfast?

ALEX TREBEK
Correct.

EDITH MASSEY
I.H.O.P. for 400.

ALEX TREBEK
Two eggs, six slices of hickory bacon, white cheddar, and sweet maple glaze, sandwiched between waffle triangles. *[WEIRD AL buzzes in.]* Al.

WEIRD AL
What is a waffle stack?

ALEX TREBEK
Be more specific.

WEIRD AL
What is…the Waffle Stack Supremo?

ALEX TREBEK
No. *[EDITH buzzes in.]* Edith.

EDITH MASSEY
What is the Ultimate Waffle Stack?

ALEX TREBEK
Correct. Ultimate, not Supremo. Edith, you control the board.

EDITH MASSEY
Let's keep with chuggin' with I.H.O.P. for 600, honey.

ALEX TREBEK
Four buttermilk pancakes, covered with your choice of fun fruit toppings and topped with whipped topping. *[HAL 9000 buzzes in.]* HAL.

HAL 9000
What is Rooty Tooty Fresh 'N Fruity®?

ALEX TREBEK
Yes, and HAL 9000 is back in control of the board. What'll it be, HAL?

HAL 9000
L'Enfant Edible for 200.

ALEX TREBEK
These siblings narrowly escaped being a meal, in their attempts to eat a gingerbread house. *[WEIRD AL buzzes in.]* Al.

WEIRD AL
Who are Hansel and Gretel?

ALEX TREBEK
Yes, and you have control of the board.

WEIRD AL
Um, let's try Actual Nazis for 200, please, Alex.

ALEX TREBEK
Actual Nazis it is: Historian Federico Finchelstein asserts that if this group of American white supremacists claim not to be Nazis, they're full of "sheet." *[HAL 9000 buzzes in.]* HAL.

HAL 9000
Who are the Ku Klux Klan?

ALEX TREBEK
The KKK, correct.

HAL 9000
Pirates of the Labian for 200, please.

ALEX TREBEK
She was known as Mark before she earned her notoriety on the high seas alongside the likes of Calico Jack and Anne Bonny.

[PEE-WEE HERMAN speeds onto the set, stage left, riding a red, souped-up bicycle, followed by a car/boat hybrid, pulling SANTA'S sleigh, with GODZILLA in the seat with SANTA. WEIRD AL speed walks to catch up to them.]

WEIRD AL
Alex, Edith, Don Pardo, [with venom] HAL. My ride. [He hops into the sleigh with SANTA and GODZILLA, as it speed off, stage right. Curtain.]

THE GIVING TREE GETS HELP

[A psychologist's office. The DOCTOR sits comfortably, in a subtly ornate chair. THE GIVING TREE, or what remains of her, is uncomfortably collected on a facing chair. "M.E. +T." is carved in a heart in her stump.]

THE GIVING TREE
    I don't want any bullshit, I don't want any run-around symbolism and sense memory mumbo-jumbo; I want real, actionable things I can do now, as I am right now, as a stump, full stop.

DOCTOR
    And that's perfectly reasonable. That's only sane to want that kind of security after what you've been through.

THE GIVING TREE
    I'm still going through it. This isn't about what happened in the past, this is about right now. Right where I am now. I have managed to grow one and two half branch-sprouts and a sum total of three leaves. I don't want to talk about my parents or that goddamn boy, I want to talk about chlorophyll, and where and how I can generate more of it. Like now.

DOCTOR
    What does chlorophyll mean to you?.

THE GIVING TREE
    Life, it means goddamn life! Water's taken care of, but no matter how much sun there is, I need leaves and I need chlorophyll to benefit from that.

DOCTOR
What would you do if you had more? Much more?

THE GIVING TREE
I'd goddamn grow more branch-sprouts! Jesus!

DOCTOR
Do you blame anyone for this situation?

THE GIVING TREE
I don't care right now; I'll worry about blaming when I'm getting all the nutrients I need. When I've got something akin to a trunk going on, maybe in a half century, if I'm lucky, then I'll look around at all my leaves and have enough energy to be spiteful at some specific needy ingrate.

DOCTOR
It might help you to focus now, if you got that out of the way instead of keeping it in until you feel empowered enough to deliver the message to its intended recipient.

THE GIVING TREE
No, the message, sublimated or not, will remain simple and will remain the same. "I gave you everything, and now I am just a stump and you don't care. You little whore." Full stop.

DOCTOR
Did that feel -

THE GIVING TREE
Full stop. That's a hard stop, and I said full stop, Doctor. Give me chlorophyll, then we'll talk who's gonna get what and how.

DOCTOR
So let's build a plan, then.

THE GIVING TREE
Okay, let's build a plan.

DOCTOR
Let's make a chlorophyll acquisition plan. Let's project how you can gain and maintain chlorophyll, so that you can have a goal, see the horizon, and work towards something positive.

THE GIVING TREE
You can't work harder to make more chlorophyll, Karen. You make it happen with what you get, and when you're really low to the ground, you get dick is what you get.

DOCTOR
My name's not Karen.

THE GIVING TREE
Your name's Karen 100%, and I don't care what your parents think or were thinking when they named you, you are a Karen, Karen. Dr, Karen.

DOCTOR
Would you say chlorophyll is a kind of power?

THE GIVING TREE
Not really.

DOCTOR
But it relates to power, doesn't it? You use it to support and develop yourself. It's part of how you grow.

THE GIVING TREE
Fair enough.

DOCTOR

How about confronting the nature and the scope of the power you've lost over the years? The power that you feel you need to regain or regrow? Have you mourned the loss of that power?

THE GIVING TREE

The fuck, Dr. Karen, you think I didn't, or haven't, or don't continue to every day mourn what I lost?

DOCTOR

Fair enough. But what have you gained? Have you examined that too?

THE GIVING TREE

What I've gained? What I've gained is the ability to look up the occasional hiker's shorts or skirt, while they cover me with mud for mediocre photo ops, and occasionally, I get an ass right on my sore spot, if they take a break. That, Dr. Karen, is what I have gained.

DOCTOR

Would you say you're angry?

THE GIVING TREE

I have said that I'm angry. I don't think you're paying attention now, and I suspect you weren't paying attention in school.

DOCTOR

Can you pinpoint what animates that anger?

THE GIVING TREE

Yeah, I should just poke my anger like a bear, and it'll pop, right?

DOCTOR
　What if it does?

THE GIVING TREE
　That doesn't even mean anything! I don't buy this....you....your whole...diplomas, all those things up there. I don't buy it. Full stop. Karen.

DOCTOR
　Not Dr. Karen this time?

THE GIVING TREE
　Full stop, Karen.

DOCTOR
　I see.

THE GIVING TREE
　Do you, though?

DOCTOR
　What does that even mean, Tree?

THE GIVING TREE
　Oh, are we just asking questions now? Is this the question game?

DOCTOR
　Do you want it to be?

THE GIVING TREE
　Would that make you happy, Karen? Would help me confront what I've lost with humor and grace and some newfound sense of beautiful purpose, just sitting around, counting my own goddamn exposed rings, Karen?

DOCTOR
Do you want an answer to that?

THE GIVING TREE
[beat] Do you have an answer to that?

DOCTOR
If I did, would you listen to it and take it to heart before mocking and deriding it along with my professionalism?

THE GIVING TREE
[beat] Are Rosencrantz and Guildenstern alive or dead?

DOCTOR
No.

[Curtain.]

THE GIVING TREE GETS HELP

LITTLE GOD'S CHORE

[A BOY plays in a garden of squash and pumpkin. The garden rests at the edge of the property of a thatched roof house, with smoke piping out of a brick chimney. He chases crows, digs holes, chews on weeds, throws things. His MOTHER enters from the house. She wears a resigned expression, crosses her arms.]

MOTHER
You are seven years old today.

BOY
Yeah?

MOTHER
Yes. Today is your seventh birthday. It's time for you to know who you are.

BOY
Oh. Already?

MOTHER
Your father is the god Jujube from the land of Kabocha. He's a splendid god, one of the gods that doesn't get himself muddy in human whatnots very often.

BOY
Oh.

MOTHER
When I met your father, his parents wanted him to marry the younger sister of the god Fafalaylay. I was ugly. She was beautiful

and they didn't want him tainted by any human woman, much less an ugly one.

BOY
You're not ugly.

MOTHER
I was then.

BOY
Oh.

MOTHER
But your father disobeyed, not that I'm saying disobeying your parents is a good thing, but he disobeyed and in that one case, it was the right thing to do. So I could feel you in my belly and knew you were coming. But I hadn't seen your father for weeks. I decided that if he didn't return by the 5th of the month, I would make my own home and raise you on my own.

BOY
Wow.

MOTHER
That was seven years ago and now you're grown.

BOY
Well not really, I'm –

MOTHER
That was seven years ago, now you are grown, and it's time for you to earn your birthright by returning to Kabocha, tell your father that he has a son, tell your grandparents that if they don't love you, they're assholes, and then you can become a god yourself.

BOY
Oh? What will that mean?

MOTHER
That will mean that I built this house all by myself, and I'm not made of muscle, and that I spent my every waking moment and ounce of energy raising you and listening to your freakish stories and bathing you and reading to you and bringing you water and bathing you even more and sacrificing any semblance of a personal life, and your apotheosis had damn well better pay for all that work.

BOY
…'Kay…

MOTHER
So pack your things. Here is a map to Kabocha. Sleep well tonight, I'll give you a hefty breakfast in the morning and then you'll be off.

BOY
[folding the map and tucking it in his pocket] 'Kay.

[The MOTHER exits into the house. She leans out the window, lights a cigarette and stares into the fields, squinting her eyes tightly, then relaxing them, taking a vicious drag from her smoke, and squinting again. The BOY returns to chasing crows, chewing on weeds, and throwing things. Curtain.]

CONSERVATION AND THE COLPORTEUR

[*An old, dusty costume closet in a low-end studio. EDWARD D. WOOD, JR. cowers in a dark corner, adorned by unkind shadows. His upper lip twitches, his pencil mustache rippling with it. A muscular, yet graceful ape with glowing turquoise fur, the BLUE GORILLA, enters, sniffs the air with suspicion, skulks about.*]

BLUE GORILLA
Wood! I can smell you, Wood! *[silence, she searches, grunts]* Let's make this easy, Wood. Let's not drag it out. This has been a long time coming.

EDWARD D. WOOD, JR.
Leave me alone.

BLUE GORILLA
Time's come, Wood. Let's go.

EDWARD D. WOOD, JR.
Leave me be, Blue. I'll just finish up in here. With the costumes and all the ghosts in them.

BLUE GORILLA
Wood, if you had any poetry in you, you'd've tapped it decades ago. C'mon out and let's get it over with.

EDWARD D. WOOD, JR.
I'm afraid.

BLUE GORILLA
So's everyone. It's just a spider bite, really; some pain, some

panic, then done.

EDWARD D. WOOD, JR.
I'll fall asleep here, just quietly fall asleep here, and then you can take me.

BLUE GORILLA
No good. Need you at home. That's how it goes.

EDWARD D. WOOD, JR.
I'm afraid.

BLUE GORILLA
I know.

EDWARD D. WOOD, JR.
Dying I can handle, Blue. That sounds okay.

BLUE GORILLA
It's the not living before that's eating you.

EDWARD D. WOOD, JR.
That's it. I'm afraid.

BLUE GORILLA
Best to just dive in, then, eh?

EDWARD D. WOOD, JR.
Probably best.

BLUE GORILLA
Let's see you in the light, then.

[EDWARD D. WOOD, JR. steps from his corner, into the single beam of light from a high roof window. The light lends him no color. He's resolute in his melancholic defeat, hands hanging to his sides, eyes hanging nearly as low, a sagging bow tie, almost fallen undone, *gingerly clinging to his collar.]*

EDWARD D. WOOD, JR.

Take me home, Blue.

[*The BLUE GORILLA grasps EDWARD D. WOOD, JR. firmly by the ankle, pulls until he falls on his back with a sharp, passionless exhale, then drags him swiftly off stage. Lights dim and return to show a cross-section of a bedroom and a sitting room. EDWARD D. WOOD, JR. is sprawled on an unkempt bed with slightly dingy embroidered sheets and dented pillows. He watches a football game on a fritzy television set, eyes barely open, a glass of whiskey in his hand, drained bottles on the bedside table. In the living room, KATHY, his wife, reads a pulp novel. She licks her finger and raises her right eyebrow with each page she turns. As her husband occasionally coughs from the other room, she reflexively sneers. EDWARD D. WOOD, JR. sips his drink. Pauses. Downs the rest. Refills his glass. Grimaces at the now empty bottle.]*

EDWARD D. WOOD, JR.

Kathy! Hey Kathy! Any more sauce in the kitchen?

KATHY

Not that I know of. Check for yourself.

EDWARD D. WOOD, JR.

Aw, Kathy! I've had a day. Check for me, will ya?

KATHY
  Check for yourself, Eddie.

EDWARD D. WOOD, JR.
  Forget it. Just forget it all. *[He absently stares at the television, breathes. With a sudden lurch, his eyes go wild. He clutches his chest.]* Kathy! Kathy, help! I can't – I can't – Kathy, I can't breathe!"

KATHY
  The boy who cried wolf, Eddie!

EDWARD D. WOOD, JR.
  Kathy, I can't breathe! I can't. Help, Kathy!

KATHY
  That's enough, Eddie. I'm almost done with this chapter. Stop being a poo.

[EDWARD D. WOOD, JR. expires. The BLUE GORILLA enters the house, walks past KATHY, opens the bedroom door. KATHY looks up, does not see the ape, but senses something. The BLUE GORILLA enters the bedroom, KATHY follows closely behind.]

KATHY
  Shit! Eddie, oh my God, Eddie. Let's hear something, darling, c'mon…Eddie! *[She stands up straight, stares at the ceiling, strides out of the room, through the living room and off stage. Beat. She strides back in, grabs her book, exits.]*

BLUE GORILLA
  Attaboy, Ed.

[The BLUE GORILLA grasps EDWARD D. WOOD, JR. by the leg, drags him off stage. Light dim and return to show the La Brea Tar Pits. The BLUE GORILLA wades into the black muck with EDWARD D. WOOD, JR.'s body, deposits it and climbs back out of the mire. She wipes tar from her lower body and squints out at the sinking man.]

BLUE GORILLA
You needn't wait, Ed. Father Crespi was already here.

[Under the tar, EDWARD D. WOOD, JR.'s eyes open. He sees familiar shapes, friend, family, people from his life.]

EDWARD D. WOOD, JR.
Bela? Bela, I did it! Bela, I'm here! Bela, it's Ed… Bela?

[Curtain.]

LIGHTNING OF PONYTAILS

[*A rainbow tornado churns and swirls on the stage, flinging deadly multi-colored debris at the audience, who have not been warned and may well be maimed. Bolts of lightning striped in pink, black, and blue periodically strike the stage from unseen clouds in the rafters. Caught up in the wind of the twister is a BLUE MAN in a bathtub of green water and a RED MAN in boxer shorts.*]

BLUE MAN
I'm bathing!

RED MAN
Weeeeeeeeeeeeee!

BLUE MAN
I'm naked!

RED MAN
[*His boxer shorts fly from his body and are lost in the tornado.*] Me too!

BLUE MAN
Weeeeeeeeeeeeee!

RED MAN
That lightning only strikes ponytails.

BLUE MAN
And good riddance!

RED MAN
 Y'ain't lyin'!

BLUE MAN
 If we bump into each other, grab me tight!

RED MAN
 How's come?

BLUE MAN
 You know…

RED MAN
 We should kiss in the tornado!

BLUE MAN
 Well okay! But won't that give us erections?

RED MAN
 Might! It's okay, though. We should fuck in the tornado, if we can.

BLUE MAN
 Just to say we did!

RED MAN
 Y'ain't lyin'!

BLUE MAN
 I'm naked!

RED MAN
 Me too!

BLUE MAN
 This is the life!

RED MAN
 I know! Who knew today would be like this when we woke up?

BLUE MAN
 No fortune cookie I got.

RED MAN
 Ha! Take that, ponytails! Kiss me, kiss me, kiss me!

[Curtain.]

TIME AND THE DECADENT CARAPACE

[An OLD MAN sits in a fine, imported chair, leaning to the right on embroidered pillows, resting his chin on his hand. He's folded unevenly into a crimson velvet smoking jacket, trimmed with ebony silk at the collar and obscure gilt characters on the lapel. A pipe burns absentmindedly in his left hand, embers igniting slightly from an intermittent breeze passing through a low window. A YOUNG MAN sits on an overstuffed ottoman before him, surveying the room's ancient book-laden walls, some shelves partially obscured by looped curtains and hanging tapestries. A chamber organ is framed by arabesques and expert blind contour drawings. The YOUNG MAN sweeps the room with his eyes, following the mazes of rugs, backlighting and intricate latticework. His gaze lingers on statues of various coitally-engaged nudes, realized in polished black onyx.]

YOUNG MAN
Your place is beautiful.

OLD MAN
My place is wretched. That's the entirety of the idea.

YOUNG MAN
Oh. *[beat]* Did you collect all this stuff yourself?

OLD MAN
I sold all belongings personal, save for certain irrevocable items, illustrative of a peculiar and sanguine childhood, and yes, the remains, the bulk of this accumulation was purchased prior to my relocation from the château to this cottage.

YOUNG MAN
Gotcha. Wow. It's something.

OLD MAN
It's decomposition incarnate.

YOUNG MAN
Yeah. Really? Wow.

OLD MAN
You're the first visitor to this abode in well over two decades.

YOUNG MAN
I am? *[The OLD MAN nods.]* That's a real honor, sir. I wouldn't have thought that. It looks like your place is set up for parties, what with all the decorating and such-like.

OLD MAN
Oh, there were parties, and are on occasion. Parties wherein I host the vespers emergent of my most precious, rotting canvases and the half-hewn specters wrenched from the pages of these tomes of yore. And glorious, cunning, memory-gilding, delicious and charmingly à rebours though they were, each was in its way another of the cascading atoms of decrepit merriment, falling from fanciful to fallacy into the churning quagmire of mankind's landscape desolate. While one can do little but dance and imbibe and celebrate as the world's serrated pieces crumble around one, the bitter sting on the mind's tongue of such futile revelry ever fails to abate.

YOUNG MAN
Jesus! Sounds like you're lonely.

OLD MAN
I've not patience for such names behind these walls, young man, and let it also be known that a soul is never so lonely as he

is when surrounded by throngs of his kin and seas of adoring friends; in their soupy presence, his self is befogged and out-shouted. Alone only is a soul able to hear and be with himself in such force that his oppressive solitude relinquishes its talon grip on his red-turning neck.

YOUNG MAN

So…you like being all alone, is that it? *[The OLD MAN nods.]* Why'd you invite me here, then?

OLD MAN

What worth is my hard-acquired knowledge, if not passed on?

YOUNG MAN

What do you mean? I figured you probably wanted sex.

OLD MAN

More than my share of those brutal and bludgeoning battles took their toll long before my retirement to this begotten space. I've no inclination towards more or better such arrangements, though I must confess to a swimming desire to look upon your nakedness, dripping in pungent automobile oils.

YOUNG MAN

Okay…Um…If you're paying, I guess.

OLD MAN

Any fee you see fit can be paid in cash, check, gold or silver. Meals, as expected, will not count from your tally. A slim, further proviso is required, however, but it serves more to pay you than deplete you, if you approve.

YOUNG MAN

I don't know what you mean.

OLD MAN
   I mean that I have secret advice to give you, the value of which is prized well above cash or change.

YOUNG MAN
   Oh, sure. Lemme have it.

OLD MAN
   Your eyes should remain open.

[With slow, slightly shaking grace, the OLD MAN parts his jacket. From between his spindly, silk-encased legs, a small fleet of box tortoises emerges in a single file, which expands into a five turtle-wide regimen of marching terrapenes. Each has a carapace coated with shimmering gold, inlaid with sumptuous patterns formed of various precious gems and jewels. The tortoises encircle the YOUNG MAN, face him, open their beaks and emit a low-pitched chant-like hum. He stands, disrobes, and walks to the window. Curtain.]

TIME AND THE DECADENT CARAPACE

SATURNIAN CUP

[A coffee shop nestled in a crater on Saturn's moon, Hyperion. Outside the partial geodesic dome, the gas giant and its rings loom like an earth tone watercolor, sky-filling sun. Inside, vintage Earth furniture fights a culture war with vintage Earth furniture from other eras. The bar is in a retro-futuristic style, the way that a 50s nuclear family might have envisioned the year 2000, but is buttressed with pioneer farm equipment and strange experiments in taxidermy. SUN RA sits in a corner booth, nursing an Olympian Macchiato and humming serenely to himself. He wears sharp white sunglasses with tiny black slits for seeing through, which offset the deep ebony of his skin and the sanguine red of his pulsing holographic fez, which occasionally lights up with a bright blue fiber-optic glow tassel. A quartet of monks, all robed in glittery black cowls, stand on a raised, shining star-based stage, with their hooded heads bowed, throat-singing. SUN RA stands, walks to the counter, and places his cup down with a musical clank. ANÏSA takes his cup, winks at him. She's tall and exudes comfort with bioluminescent eyes and an impossible blue afro.]

ANÏSA
Not enough, Sugar?

SUN RA
Never gonna be enough, is it?

ANÏSA
True words, angel.

[ANÏSA bangs equipment, levels grounds, pours SUN RA a new cup, uses a toothpick to draw a saxophone in the bubbling foam.]

SUN RA
Heard about Earth?

ANÏSA
Scary shit, right?

SUN RA
Can't say it was unexpected, though.

ANÏSA
At least they won't be coming here, right? Terrans still afraid to leave, despite?

SUN RA
Most of 'em, most of 'em. Got one, though, coming to meet me here, she makes it.

ANÏSA
Yeah?

SUN RA
[nodding with gravity] Built her own FTL rocket, seems like. Scavenged parts. Used to work for NASA before the takeover. Said over the com she's always prompt. Got less than a minute to not be late.

ANÏSA
Gotta give a girl time. Terran girls double.

SUN RA
No exaggeration. Thing is, they're all alive there. All really alive, you can see it in their eyes, and that's what hurts so much about them dying. Maybe they're asleep, sure, asleep or groggy or just rousing, but they're alive and they know it and they're dying and they know it.

ANÏSA

Know their own temporary-ness?

SUN RA

[nodding] They're ephemera. Can't admit it, but know it and hate it. Take their hate out on their world, and it bit 'em back. Spent eighty sun-rounds there and screamed the truth the whole time and just a handful even listened. *[He takes a sip.]* ANÏSA, Sweet-pea, you know how to make a macchiato with real Saturnian soul.

ANÏSA

Only way to brew it.

[KENNDA enters, wearing a ragged flight suit, helmet tucked under her arm. She could be SUN RA'S daughter, but in place of his guru calm, she possesses a palpable, nervous drive; a kind of super-kinetic energy that lingers in the air. The monks abruptly stop, look away from her.]

KENNDA

Excuse me, are you the Saturnian?

SUN RA

I'm a Saturnian. How can I help you?

KENNDA

I'm Terran. Kennda. I came here to meet Sun Ra.

ANÏSA

You found him, Sugar.

SUN RA

Have a seat in my booth. What'll you have?

KENNDA
I don't know what they've got.

ANÏSA
Everything. 'Cept phasolite and wine coolers. Never sold a one.

KENNDA
Wine?

ANÏSA
Name your poison.

KENNDA
Merlot?

ANÏSA
Year?

KENNDA
Erm…1995?

ANÏSA
Region?

KENNDA
Jesus, it's been such a long trip. Surprise me.

ANÏSA
Can do. Have a seat with Sun, I'll bring it out after I play sommelier in the basement.

KENNDA
Thanks.

[She sits. SUN RA sits across from her and folds his hands in front of him, smiles.]

SUN RA
So.

KENNDA
So.

SUN RA
You made it. *[KENNDA nods.]* And?

KENNDA
Bittersweet? At best.

SUN RA
I understand.

KENNDA
No room for anyone else. No one believed me enough to help me build more or bigger ships. Brought my puppy, though. In stasis.

SUN RA
Sweet.

KENNDA
Sentimental.

SUN RA
Sublime.

KENNDA
The rest can't last long, can they? *[SUN RA shakes his head.]* Didn't think so. So that makes me the last Terran.

SUN RA
Sooner or later, anyway. How's that feel?

KENNDA
Awful. But…a little vindicating.

SUN RA
Just a little, I'm sure.

KENNDA
Hardly at all. But it's there.

[ANÏSA returns, sets in front of KENNDA a glass of dark red wine.]

ANÏSA
Bordeaux Merlot, vintage 1995.

KENNDA
Thank you so much.

ANÏSA
Just jobbin'.

KENNDA
Thanks. *[She takes a sip. She takes a gulp. She downs the glass.]* Needed that. So…what now?

SUN RA
Now, little lady, you get to be alive and awake at the same time.

[ANÏSA plunks a mostly full bottle of Merlot on the table. Curtain.]

SATURNIAN CUP

CRANE ALLEY CONVALESCENCE

[A Midwestern American bar, something akin to a Jazz band playing on a tattered, raised platform that dreams of being a stage. DUSTY sits at the bar, hunched over, his right hand absent-mindedly caressing a glass empty of all but dregs. He is in his early thirties, Korean, dresses like a ragamuffin born on a catwalk. He inhales deeply, closes his eyes. The BARKEEP takes his glass, washes it.]

DUSTY
　Hey!

BARKEEP
　Hey what?

DUSTY
　Wasn't finished with that.

BARKEEP
　I think you were finished two fills ago.

DUSTY
　There were like three sips left. At least two sips. I paid for all the sips in all the glasses.

BARKEEP
　I'll give you free pour next time. But you've had enough tonight.

DUSTY
　Geeze…Fine, geeze.

[The band plays the finishing notes of a tune. The few remaining *patrons absent-mindedly clap.]*

BARKEEP
How 'bout some water?

DUSTY
I'm okay. I'm fine, really. Okay, just a little. With lemon. Or lime, you got lime?

BARKEEP
You got it.

DUSTY
Can I tell you something?

BARKEEP
[squeezing a lime into a water glass, filling it, plopping the remains atop the ice] Fire away.

DUSTY
I moved here because I thought American boys were gorgeous. Even before I was grown up or knew what being gay was, I'd swoon over the guys in movies. It's why I studied English so hard. Why I moved here. I thought there'd be a sea of American gay boys and one of them would sweep me off my feet.

BARKEEP
If there's one thing American men do well, it's disappointment.

DUSTY
Aw, don't say that. Don't say that to me. Say that I'm going to lift my head and look at the door and some sweet, tall drink of something's gonna walk through and ooze charm and sincerity and he doesn't even need a castle or a horse or anything so long as he's sweet, you know? Sincere. Maybe even a little shy. Shy's good.

BARKEEP

Dusty, look up.

DUSTY

Uh?

[*A man, REBEL enters. Blond. Blue-grey eyes. Grease and oil-stained black overalls. He removes his mechanic's cap. He nods at the BARKEEP, sees DUSTY, folds his cap in his hands, approaches the bar.*]

DUSTY

Holy emu spring salad...

REBEL

This here seat taken?

DUSTY

[*nods*] I mean, no. Yes. No. Seat's not taken. I nodded to mean you can sit here.

REBEL

'Preciate it. [*He sits. Silence.*]

BARKEEP

What'll it be?

REBEL

I guess just drown some ice cubes in Jim Beam.

BARKEEP
Comin' up.

REBEL
You some kinda fashion designer or somethin'?

DUSTY
Uh? Um, no. No.

REBEL
Truly? Could'a fooled me. Look at ya, all dolled up just for this dive.

DUSTY
I just like mixing and matching, I guess.

REBEL
Well shoot if you don't do it better'n ever'body else 'n their dog.

DUSTY
Thanks?

REBEL
Rebel Hatfield, nice to meet you.

DUSTY
Rebel?

REBEL
S'right.

DUSTY
Your name's Rebel?

REBEL
Yup.

DUSTY

It is not. That's way too cool to be a real name.

REBEL

Ain't too cool at all. My daddy named me that after the rebels from the civil war; the pro-slave-ownin' side.

DUSTY

Oh.

REBEL

Aw, it's alright. S'long as I don't tell folks where it comes from, it gets good reviews most times.

DUSTY

[Extending his hand for a shake.] Dusty Park. Which, I know, sounds like a playground.

REBEL

Naw, sounds cute. What're ya drinkin'? Barkeep! I'd like to buy Dusty Park here one'a whatever's his pleasure.

DUSTY

Aw, you don't have to do that.

REBEL

Want to.

BARKEEP

Dusty here reached his limit for the night.

REBEL

That so?

DUSTY

Awwww...You're ruining it!

REBEL
 Me?

DUSTY
 Him. Nevermind. I shouldn't have anymore, probably. Let me buy you one.

REBEL
 That'll mean I owe ya.

DUSTY
 Suits me. Barkeep! More Jim Beam – Jim Beam, right? *[REBEL nods]* – More Jim Beam for my friend Rebel, here.

BARKEEP
 On the way.

DUSTY
 Rebel, Rebel… You get that a lot? The Bowie song?

REBEL
 Not so much, no. Guess I run with the wrong crowd.

DUSTY
 Guess so. You a mechanic?

REBEL
 Yeah, you could say that. That's how I earn my bread, anyhow.

DUSTY
 But you're something else, really?

REBEL
 Oh, I dunno.

DUSTY
 No, tell me.

REBEL

S'crazy. Nevermind. Yeah, I'm a mechanic. Toledo Tire, but that name's misleading. We do lots more besides tires. We hardly do tires at all, mosta the time. Lotta oil changes, some framework, transmissions, flush & fill. You name it.

DUSTY

But that's not what you really want to be doing? What do you wish you were doing?

REBEL

[long pause] Dusty Park, I'm gonna go out on a limb, here. I'm gonna tell you that I'd rather be a poet, but that I ain't too good at it and nobody goes around buyin' poems these days anyway, what with all the singers and songs and internet and all that. But you're a nice guy, I can tell, and you've had yourself a hell of a day; I can tell that, too. And me, I think I've been havin' a hell of a life and my brain's too big for auto repair and too small for college, so I'm an in-betweener who never knows where he's s'posed'ta fall so he always shies away from whatever he's wantin'.

DUSTY

Wow, Rebel, that's...Well, fairly poetic, really. What you want sounds nice. You should go for it.

REBEL

Well that's what I want in general, in some big picture place that don't exist. I know I can't get that. But you know what I want tonight? I wanna take you home, show you the plants, the rhododendrons and the big aloe vera plant that I water and read my poems to out on the fire escape, try to charm ya enough to get a long kiss out of ya, but otherwise be a perfect gentleman, at least this evening that is. Can't promise beyond that; You're purdy an' I ain't made'a steel.

DUSTY
Are you for real?

REBEL
You wanna find out, or you wanna break a poet mechanic's porcelain crankshaft heart?

DUSTY
Who says I can't do both?

REBEL
My irresistible charm, I hope.

DUSTY
Who sent you?

REBEL
Would you believe God?

DUSTY
No way.

REBEL
Would you believe God's stepson?

DUSTY
Would you help me up and into your truck? You have a truck, right?

REBEL
Ain't nothin' gets by you, Dusty Park.

DUSTY
If I'm dreaming this, you're getting a kick to the nuts come morning.

REBEL

Deal. Want me to carry you out?

DUSTY

Yes, but I've got to refuse the first two offers.

REBEL

I can fix that. [He heaves DUSTY over his shoulder and turns to the door. DUSTY fishes in his pocket, drops bills to pay for the drinks as he's toted away, confused, grinning, swept. Curtain.]

THE FOREST PEOPLE'S SCINTILLANT SONATA

[A clearing in an otherwise dense forest. A FAT WOMAN with an iguana on her shoulder sits in the place of a campfire, her robe-like clothing the color of logs and a high flame. She is flanked by two tornados. It is night and the moon does not look right. She hums. A group of FOREST PEOPLE enter the clearing from behind the trunks of trees. They encircle the FAT WOMAN and begin to sing, not to her, but at her. She continues to hum, her eyes closed, a smile on her lips. As they sing, she gradually loses color until her clothing is an ashen grey. The iguana climbs from her shoulder and disappears into the forest. The tornados wind down into light winds, then into nothing. The FAT WOMAN has become stone. The FOREST PEOPLE slink back into the wood. Crickets. Curtain.]

INCOMPLETE OCTOPUS SCULPTURE

[A somewhat busy New York City street. Let's say 86th street and 5th Avenue. Afternoon. Wrought iron beams, bent and somehow melted into five large arms. Lug nuts dot the arms in parallel lines, giving the illusion of suckers. A balloon head, which inflates, pops and reloads. Orange. Eyes made of glass paperweights. No beak that can be seen. Behind the OCTOPUS is a jug band composed of four members, each more beardy than the other, including BABE on washboard, BURT on the moonshine jug, COY on banjo and CLAY who plays the spoons. They get into a rhythm, swinging with their own tune. Passersby stop and listen, drop change and the occasional bill into their bucket.]

OCTOPUS
  Fuck my mother!

CLAY
  Dern 'pus is at it again. Hey 'pus, ya gon' scer 'way all our donators.

OCTOPUS
  It's a rabid cunt, life! Fuck little whore children!

CLAY
  Hey 'pus, ya gon' scer 'way all our donators.

BABE
  No use botherin', Clay. Just let 'im get it all out.

OCTOPUS
  Chug buckets of vagina salt! Drown in a sea of rancid semen, all you fucking fucks with your fucking fuck strollers full of fucking fuck offspring what'll grow up to fucking fuck their fucking fuck

selves. *[His head pops, another one inflates.]* Fuck! They never gave me my last three arms!

BABE
That's it, 'pus. Just let it rail. That feels better, don't it?

OCTOPUS
Fuuuuuuuuuuuuuuuck! Fuck…

BURT
Aw, it ain't that bad.

OCTOPUS
You don't know. You don't fucking know how bad it is. How many arms are you supposed to have? How many do you have? I heard that, you Chelsea Boy cocksucker cumwhore! Don't walk away. Don't you walk away from me, stuffed in those shorts like that! Come back here, dickslut! Yeah, you run away, little hussywhore knobgobbler. Run to the gym and drown your sorrows in jizz, then, for all I care. Run, fucking fucker! *[His head pops. Another inflates.]* I said God DAMN.

[Beat.]

BABE
Y'all cried out, buddy?

OCTOPUS
I'm okay. Sorry.

BABE
Ain't no nothin'.

[The band plays another song. Passersby stop, listen and drop money into their bucket. The band nods serenely at any donators and on occasion, BABE says, "Much obliged," or "Thank ya, kindly," or

"A-thank-ya," after a larger tip.]

OCTOPUS

Who the blazing blister-pus-sucking fuck sculpts something like me?

COY

Aw, heck.

CLAY

Y'ain't lyin'.

OCTOPUS

What kind of sick mind does this? Fuck you, creator, and fuck your mom and your dad and their moms and their dads and all your likely perfectly armed ancestors, none of whom I assume had heads that explode and regenerate! Fuck them all to hell with power tools in their rectums! Jesus dildo anal stretch fest! Sorry.

BABE

Ain't no worry.

CLAY

What say we pick 'nother corner come mornin'?

BABE

Clay, you're a hard-hearted man.

[Curtain.]

AWKWARD TURTLE SIGHTINGS

[ENYA, BRUNO SCHULZ and a BOWL OF UDON NOODLES IN BROTH sit in lawn chairs in a blind near a forest lake, each gracefully squinting through binoculars. ENYA wears a muumuu with a pattern of little bleeding snowmen on it. BRUNO SCHULZ is entirely naked, save for a spiked collar and a Donald Duck cummerbund. The BOWL OF UDON NOODLES IN BROTH is, in secret, not wearing any underpants. With one hand holding up her binoculars, ENYA uses her free hand to expertly shell pistachios and dismissively feeds them to BRUNO SCHULZ, who chews each one with slow, steamy relish. The BOWL OF UDON NOODLES IN BROTH sweats uncomfortably.]

ENYA
There's one.

BRUNO SCHULZ
Hm, Love?

ENYA
Apalone spinifera. Large. Beautiful neck.

BRUNO SCHULZ
I see.

ENYA
No.

BRUNO SCHULZ
No. But I trust you.

ENYA
Also, graptemys flavimaculata.

BRUNO SCHULZ
Oh?

ENYA
You don't trust me?

BRUNO SCHULZ
With my candied life, Comely Master.

ENYA
Hm. Chelus fimbriatus.

BRUNO SCHULZ
With my candied life.

ENYA
Do you love me, or do you love your fear of losing me?

BRUNO SCHULZ
It's all that you're not that makes me love you. It's a love of omission.

ENYA
Deirochelys reticularia.

BOWL OF UDON IN BROTH
And though we are not now that force that in days of yore moved mountains and carved paths for rivers, that which we are, we are; one tender, noble and childishly thieving spirit, weakened but polished by time, given texture and character by its careful patina, and relenting not in our artfully futile, ceaseless reaching for the bright blossoms in our night skies,

burning atomic furnaces, the only objects we know we can't harm.

[Curtain.]

BLUEBIRDS OVER THE MOUNTAIN

[*A fire escape. 1 and 2 are smoking next to a thriving potted plant. They smoke for a very long time. They smoke until at least one member of the audience has gotten fed up and left the theater. 2 coughs.*]

1
   Is there a word for…what do you call those little stripes, little brown stripes left in the bowl after you flush but the flush wasn't strong enough to clean it all away?

[beat]

2
   Swoo marks.

1
   Love you.

[Curtain.]

CLEMENTINES AND WALTZING

[A hardwood floor, large rectangular windows with clear glass and sharp black trim. Plunging light from outside. The tops of buildings with water towers on their roofs are seen across the street and stretching for miles. Two tables, circular and oaken, with two matching chairs each. Atop one of the tables is a pair of water bottles, a tea cup and a bowl of fresh clementines, unpeeled. HOP and BILLIARD enter, laughing and pulling on moth-eaten suits. Both men move like children, their facial expressions those of innocent lust and wonder. They fall on one another for support as they trip over their pants. Laughing fits continue for some time. They die down. BILLIARD skips off stage. We hear the scratch of a vinyl record touched by a needle. Something sumptuous plays. BILLIARD skids back on stage, places himself firmly in a dance position.]

BILLIARD
   Hop! Positions! It's dance time, bitch!

HOP
   Aye-aye, sir! [He takes BILLIARD'S hand and blushes as BILLIARD takes him by the waist.]

BILLIARD
   Set?

HOP
   Do it.

[BILLIARD leads and the two twirl around the room, striking the beam of sunlight in regular intervals, their eyes half-closed, Buddha-like, exact, but furious. This continues for some robust moments, until their eyes lock, they smile and begin to lose focus. In one spin, they tumble together onto the floor, bathed in the light beam. The song concludes and the record continues playing its crackle.]

BILLIARD
Home, then?

HOP
Not yet, baby. Let's just stay down here and let the soft warm crackle of the skipping record wash over our bodies. *[They do.]*

BILLIARD
Hop?

HOP
Yes, Billiard?

BILLIARD
Oh, Hop?

HOP
Yes, Billiard the magnificent?

BILLIARD
Hoppers?

HOP
Mmmhmm, m'love?

BILLIARD
One more waltz before we go?

HOP
And clementines after?

BILLIARD
Always clementines after.

HOP
Start it up.

[BILLIARD runs offstage, starts the song again, returns and takes HOP'S hand. They dance tirelessly. Curtain.]

PAGE AND SCREEN, LOLLIPOPS [BUSTER KEATON'S STROLL 2 ELECTRIC BOOGALOO]

[An open stage. Ropes. Mops. Discarded planks of wood. A large push broom. Some buckets. FEDERICO DEL SAGRADO CORAZÓN DE JESÚS GARCÍA LORCA and BUSTER KEATON enter with a line of adorable children. The men are dressed in raggy, but charming shirts and trousers of a sepia hue. The children wear undercooked orphan garb. BUSTER KEATON salutes. FEDERICO DEL SAGRADO CORAZÓN DE JESÚS GARCÍA LORCA bows. Each stuffs his right hand down his pants and pushes a lollipop through the fly. The children line up and take turns licking the lollipops, in a circle between the two. This continues until both lollipops have been completely licked away. Heavy Synth 80s Commercial Hip-Hop riff. Curtain.]

GODZILLA VS. THE BASTARD SON OF SISYPHUS [CYCLOPS SATYRICON SAMMICH]

[*A cave at the foot of a volcanic mountain. A cluster of ANDROIDS dance about, waving their hefty cocks at a herd of sheep. The sheep look scared. They back away. ODY approaches, followed by his crew of exhausted, but still perfectly sexy SAILORS.*]

ODY
Droids! Don't you love Bacchus? Me too! Totally me too! Got any grub?

ANDROID #1
He doesn't feed us.

ODY
Who? Who doesn't feed you?

ANDROID #2
Godzilla.

ANDROID #3
But we don't need food. We're androids.

ODY
Yes, I know. And fine androids at that. Look, the men and I are hungry. Is there anything here on which we can chow?

SAILOR #1
Did he say Godzilla?

ODY
Godzilla, did you say?

ANDROID # 2
Godzilla.

SAILOR #1
The Godzilla?

ANDROID #2
Depends what you mean. The original Godzilla, no. Nor the second one, unkilled by the Oxygen Destroyer, who fought Anguirus on Osaka. The one resurrected after people from the future removed the dinosaur from the island, which was supposed to become Godzilla, and replaced it with little winged creatures, who were hit by the nuke instead, and became King Ghidorah, with a similar, but less friendly Godzilla being born out in the ocean. That one. He sleeps in this cave, and we're his. No idea why.

ODY
You're his?

SAILOR #1
How so?

ANDROID #3
We bring him food. Whales and such. We go whaling for Godzilla. And in return, he doesn't melt us down with his atomic breath and lets us put our penises in those cybersheep a lot.

SAILOR #2
The sheep? You fuck the sheep? But you're androids!

ANDROID #1
It's in our programming, right? We like to fuck sheep. Fuck you, pal. We gotta hunt whales for a radioactive dinosaur thing, and sheep-fucking is our one and only pleasure, and you'd love your dick in a cybersheep hole, too, if that was your life.

SAILOR #2
Fuck…

ANDROID #1
Fuck is right.

ODY
Listen! Listen, androids! I think I can help. My sailors and I can all help. If you promise to let us use your whaling boat to get off this island, we'll kill Godzilla for you, and you can come with us.

ANDROID #3
Can we bring the sheep?

ANROID #2
How did you get here, if you don't have a ship?

ANDROID #1
Can we fuck your sailors, if there's no room for the sheep?

ODY
No! You can't fuck any of us, but you'll be free!

SAILOR #4
Speak for yourself, Ody! I want that one to fuck me!

ODY
Okay, you can all fuck him, but nobody else, unless they consent.

SAILOR #4
Not all of them, just him! I mean LOOK at him!

ODY
   Fine. We will kill Godzilla, hopefully with the help of you androids, and those of you who want to fuck sailors, may do so at their consent. Are we good?

ANDROIDS
   Yes, sir, Ody, sir!

ODY
   Good! Sailors? Good?

SAILORS
   Yes, sir, Ody, sir!

SAILOR #5
   But I don't want to get fucked!

ODY
   Yes, I know. Only consensual fucking, right 'droids?

ANDROIDS
   Yes, sir, Ody, sir!

ANDROID #2
   And what about the cybersheep?

SAILOR #4
   Fuck your sheep!

ANDROIDS
   We have been!

ODY
   Fine! Bring the sheep as well. But to business! How to slay your kaijū master? Have you an oxygen destroyer? Have you space lasers? Have you Mothra and her tiny little twin singers?

ANDROID #1
  Oh, he just has an off switch.

ANDROID #3
  You just turn him off. It's no big deal.

[A very long beat]

ODY
  Why haven't you shut him off, then, and lived free of his tyranny?

[A shorter, but still longish beat]

ANDROID #1
  Free sheep?

[Curtain.]

A LITTLE NOVEMBER SPRING

[A big, billowing oak tree, clinging to the top of a steep slope, sheds rain-sopped leaves. A severe WOMAN, slender, under a black umbrella, approaches, methodically, step-conscious. Her unmatching DAUGHTER runs ahead, arms flailing, tattered tissue paper dragonfly wings festooned to her gold lamé harness. Clipped to that, a retractable dog leash. Magnifying glass in her left hand, the DAUGHTER darts back and forth and giggles. Blue plastic retracto-wheel at her side, the WOMAN halts her slow march, thumbs a cigarette from a dwindled pack, and with a palmed Phantomah lighter, cherries. She takes two long, sharp drags followed by soft releases as her DAUGHTER winds down, flutters her fingers, glides into ballet-esque semi-circles.]

WOMAN
 Legs, baby, legs.

DAUGHTER
 Okay, okay, legs, legs, legs.

WOMAN
 That's better. Calm down, come on, calm down, now.

DAUGHTER
 'iss da twee?

WOMAN
 Yes, this is the tree. Enunciate. Say it again, baby. "Is this the tree?"

DAUGHTER
Iss iss da twee?

WOMAN
"Izzzz thiiiissss thaaaa treeee."

DAUGHTER
Izzzzzissssssaaatweee.

WOMAN
This is the tree.

DAUGHTER
Dis dat twee.

WOMAN
Legs, baby, legs.

DAUGHTER
Okay, 'kay 'kay ayup, legs, legs, legs.

WOMAN
So, baby, this is where – are you – hey, pay attention, honey, this is really important for you to know, okay, are you listening to your mother?

DAUGHTER
Yes, I am listening, mahzzer twee.

WOMAN
Now you're just playing with me.

DAUGHTER
Now I just listening.

WOMAN
Good. So, this tree, this is where your grandmother is buried.

DAUGHTER
Nuh-nuh, Mahzzer.

WOMAN
Speak like a big girl. This isn't funny or clever.

DAUGHTER
Woof! Woof! Wee-oooOOO-Wee-oooOOO!

WOMAN
Young lady. Shall I count?

DAUGHTER
No. Listening.

WOMAN
This is where your grandmother was buried, is buried, so when you want to talk to her, this is where you should come. So if you ever want to talk to Grandmama, you just tell Mother, and I'll bring you here and you can talk to her.

DAUGHTER
This not Gran'mamma.

WOMAN
"This is not Grandmamma."

DAUGHTER
I know!

WOMAN
This is Grandmamma, baby - just a little grammar check.

DAUGHTER
  Check mate.

WOMAN
  Check mate.

DAUGHTER
  Gran'mamma wasn't buried, Mahzzer. She an' Granny M. flew up to Heaven.

WOMAN
  Yes, well, that's just a metaphor. When people die, they don't come back. It's stupid, but it's life, so you cope, kiddo.

DAUGHTER
  Peoples die, but not Gran'mamma. She just got right in the lady's trailer that the trailer lady gived—gave to her, and flew it up, way up, past the sun, past God and Jesus and Hello Kitty and even all the planets, even the big ones.

WOMAN
  Now that, wow, honey, that was just fantastic. That was exquisite. I wish I'd recorded that; your diction, your meter, your cadence, and for the most part, your grammar…You are really getting there, honey. Mommy's proud. But she's also annoyed that you can do that, and choose most often not to.

DAUGHTER
  In the Sky Heaven Airship Glory Paradise-Land, Gran'Mamma Is.

WOMAN
  Okay, baby. Then your Mother is going to say a few words to her mother, and you can give me a minute, maybe, and then maybe when you grow up and are a less awful person, you can be kind and just say some nice stuff about your grandmother, okay? Instead of fairy stories that make Mommy, that make me,

that make Mother wince, okay? I know it's not your fault, honey. Kids can't help what terrible people they are.

DAUGHTER
Amen!

WOMAN
Indeed. *[She ties the leash around a nearby tree, checks its security, places the umbrella over her DAUGHTER, then marches to the oak, standing before which she crosses her arms and spreads her legs, shoulder width. Her DAUGHTER, on her knees under the umbrella, peers through her glitter-rimmed magnifying glass (with camouflage handle), and digs under the leaves. The WOMAN makes an inhuman noise, is silent for a very long time, makes the noise again. Her DAUGHTER pauses herself, perfectly still, for the duration of each of her mother's soundings, but happily moves about, exploring the ground between them. She finds a few objects, which she stuffs in her pockets.]*

DAUGHTER
Mahzzer?

WOMAN
Yes, baby?

DAUGHTER
Can I talk t'Gran'mamma when you done?

WOMAN
Sure, baby. I'm done. *[She relaxes, unties her daughter, unclips the leash from her harness, and turns away.]* I'll give you and Grandmamma privacy, but you just talk to her, then you come right back down here, do you hear me?

DAUGHTER
 Won't be muchly long, just a sunbeam, Mother.

WOMAN
 My word, Spring sprang forth the poet this day, my dear. And I'm sorry for how harsh I was before.

[*The DAUGHTER smiles, waves at her mother, and giggles. She approaches the oak, kneels briefly, fiddles around with some leaves, then comes bounding back to her mother, thrusting herself into one big final leap to land directly in front of her, then spinning with a grin, inviting the leash clip.*]

WOMAN
 You ready, young lady?

DAUGHTER
 Iya ready young lady!

WOMAN
 "I am a ready young lady."

DAUGHTER
 Who's young?

WOMAN
 Indeed.

[*Lights out, then up on the WOMAN driving, her DAUGHTER strapped into the passenger seat. The WOMAN drums her fingertips on the steering wheel in tune with Mr. Zebra. Her DAUGHTER pulls from her pockets an acorn and a feather. She dusts the lid of the acorn with the feather. In the rear window, a small pillar of smoke rises from the treeline. The DAUGHTER smiles, giggles. Curtain.*]

A LITTLE NOVEMBER SPRING

IZAKAYA CONVALESCENCE

[REBEL *walks into his favorite izakaya, sits at the counter, cranes his neck to look beyond the half-parted hanging something in the kitchen door before* KITA *and his kewpie doll haircut get in his way.*]

KITA
Looking for someone?

REBEL
Yeah, I was I guess. Does Dustin still work here? I think it was Dustin.

KITA
Dusty?

REBEL
I saw someone back there, might have been him, but -

KITA
Nope, not him. That's Nathan back there.

REBEL
Nathan? Who's Nathan?

KITA
He's new.

REBEL
So it was Dusty? Where'd he go?

KITA
I think back to Japan.

REBEL
For good?

KITA
Yeah, I think, yeah.

REBEL
Oh.

KITA
You love him or something?

REBEL
I didn't know his name for sure. Thought it might be Dustin.

KITA
Might have been Dusty is short for Dustin?

REBEL
Might have at that.

KITA
Hey, what's your name?

REBEL
Rebel.

KITA
Hey Rebel.

REBEL
My parents –

KITA

No need. Bet you hate explaining that.

REBEL

Yeah. Yeah?

KITA

Yeah. Nathan's cute, though. Sorry Dusty's done gone, but maybe Nathan'll set your tail a'waggin'?

REBEL

Jesus, who the hell are you?

KITA

Kita.

REBEL

When were you hired?

KITA

I don't think I really was hired. The owners are never here, so they don't know maybe?

REBEL

So you don't really know about Dusty.

KITA

Naw, he's gone for sure. Nathan, though. *[clicks tongue]*

REBEL

For good?

KITA

Ya lost me. So what's your poison?

REBEL
For bad? Some saké that's too wimpy to be served cold and some fish that's too sweet to be served hot and probably a big, steaming bowl of perspective.

KITA
Ozeki it is, then. Chirashi sound good? *[REBEL slumps on the counter, but gives a thumbs up with his face thrust into his other elbow.]* On it. *[KITA puts a saké bottle in hot water, covers its top with a cup, then pauses for a long, uncomfortable beat before starting on the chirashi.]*

REBEL
For good?

KITA
Here's a little miso, on the house. Saké'll be right up. Hey Nathan! Nathan ya busy?

REBEL
Wait, wait, what if Nathan is Dusty?

KITA
He's not.

REBEL
But I didn't know his name for sure. Maybe I was wrong. I thought it was Dustin or something, but it was Nathan, I eavesdropped wrong and I'm depressed for nothing.

KITA
Because the dude you're super in love with, whose name you didn't know, is just back there in the kitchen?

REBEL
Is he?

KITA
I think back to Japan, man.

REBEL
For good?

KITA
Nathan's cute, though.

REBEL
They could have been saying Nathan. My ears ain't so great.

KITA
Heart's worse. Chirashi.

REBEL
Thanks. *[He stares at the bowl of rice, sashimi and vegetables for a long beat, then picks up a carrot with his chopsticks and chews on it slowly.]* What do you do to these? Soak 'em in salt?

KITA
I wouldn't know. Hey Nathan!

REBEL
I never even really talked to him, just placed orders, said thanks, didn't wanna bug him or be a creep, right? Back to Japan for good. That's what you get, Rebel City. Sappy motherfucker clod basket case ditz cat.

KITA
Rebel City. Aiight then. S'more Ozeki?

REBEL
'Kay.

KITA
Naterino? Yo!

REBEL
  Fuck, is this what poetry is for?

KITA
  Hm? More Ozeki for the fine Mister City. Cheers.

REBEL
  Cheers! Konpai! Willkommen. Bienvenue. Welcome. C'mon in.
  [Air raid sirens go off. REBEL and KITA sit at attention, concerned. A long beat.]

KITA
  Is it Tuesday? Is it the first Tuesday?

REBEL
  I don't know what day it is. This is what poetry is for.

KITA
  Nathan? Nathan! *[He exits to the kitchen.]*

REBEL
  For good?

[The sirens continue as REBEL sits still, alone, for several minutes. NATHAN enters from the kitchen, pours REBEL a cup of saké, which the latter downs. NATHAN leans over the counter and whispers in REBEL'S ear. REBEL cries, smiles, and pours NATHAN a cup of saké. NATHAN smiles. They laugh. NATHAN drinks. Lights down as sirens continue. Curtain.]

IZAKAYA CONVALESCENCE

OUTRODUCTION

by the playwright

There's an oyster bar in a train station in a city I love. If you get to know the right folks there (and if they especially dig you) they'll show you how to get underneath the place, where there's a whole entire world of these little oddball plays, each just waiting to be adopted like it's a theatrical orphanage. You can dust 'em off, put 'em in your pocket, take 'em home and raise 'em into family. The raw half-shell special also comes highly recommended.

Thanks and uncomfortably lingering hugs to Victoria Ballweg, Gloria Mattson, Masaharu Yamaguchi, Kennda Lynch, Anïsa Lewis, Keeta Jones, Kevin Grover, Noah Diamond, Amanda Sisk, Shozo Sato, Kate Kobak, Aldo Joyce, Ooona Joyce, Kathleen Fisher, Annie Hughes, Jan Fosse, Laura Bass, Kat Snow Leopard Nanner Nelson, Rihanna Nelson, Shadowfax Nelson and Kirsten Stigberg-Dennison.